Top 10
Ways to Defuse
Your Congregational
Time Bomb

TOP 10 WAYS TO DEFUSE YOUR CONGREGATIONAL TIME BOMB

J. Kristina Tenny-Brittian

THE PILGRIM PRESS

CLEVELAND

to BILL, KAT, SHANNON, AND BRITT

for all the ways you listen and reflect

with me and continually remind me of what's

most important in life and ministry.

The Pilgrim Press, 700 Prospect Avenue, Cleveland, Ohio 44115-1100
thepilgrimpress.com
Copyright © 2008 by Julianna Kristina Tenny-Brittian

Scripture quotations, unless otherwise noted, are from the New Revised Standard Version of the Bible, © 1989 by the Division of Christian Education of the National Council of Churches of Christ in the United States of America, and are used by permission. Changes have been made for inclusivity.

Printed in the United States of America on acid-free paper.

13   12   11   10   09   08   5   4   3   2   1

Library of Congress Cataloging-in-Publication Data

Tenny-Brittian, J. Kristina (Juliana Kristina), 1960–
    Top 10 ways to defuse your congregational time bomb / J. Kristina Tenny-Brittian.
        p. cm.
    ISBN-13: 978-0-8298-1804-8 (alk. paper)
    1. Church renewal.   2. Church growth.   I. Title: Top ten ways to defuse your congregational time bomb.   II. Title.
BV600.3.T43 2008
250—dc22   2008011411

Contents

FOREWORD

Over the past twenty years I've consulted with enough stuck and dying churches to know attempting to turn around a dying church can be deadly. The responses of most churches usually range from boredom to outright hostility. As one lady screamed at me during a consultation, *"I don't care if our church is dying. It will change over my dead body!"* Transforming an existing church is full of ticking time bombs, any one of which can scuttle the mission.

I don't know of any study regarding the percentages of success versus failure in turning a church around, but any consultant will tell you it's not very good. Too many congregations would simply rather die than make the changes necessary to regain their lost vitality.

However, one thing I do know for certain about transforming a church, once you begin the process you'd better not blink, for two reasons. On the one hand, there are always one or two people who will eat you alive if you do; and on the other you'll destroy the hopes of those who dream of a leader who can lead them out of the wilderness into a new future, which makes turnaround even harder for the next pastor. So pastors who attempt turnaround can't afford to bail out when things get a bit dicey. The problem is that turnaround doesn't happen overnight, and dogged persistence is required. So it is imperative for pastors to till the congregational soil before ringing the turnaround bell.

The last church I pastored for twenty-four years was a nine-year-old church that had grown to 250 in worship and then declined to the thirty-seven people who greeted me my first Sunday. I didn't know what I was doing back then (1968); I only knew I couldn't turn the church around by myself. So my first Sunday I cast a vision and gathered a group of dreamers who were praying for a better day. Together we formed a team that met for several months and dreamed about the future. When we took our dream to the congregation, all hell broke loose. It would have been helpful to have had this book back then; perhaps our journey through the wilderness might have been less stressful and shorter.

I've known Kris for a number of years and know she has been around the block a few times. In doing so she has collected a boat-load of wisdom. If you are contemplating turnaround you should read this book. It will save you some grief.

This is not a "how to" book about turning around a church. Instead it's about the kind of attitude and climate needed for a church to turn around. It is about how to develop an in-between culture, a safe space, in which a successful turnaround has time to germinate. In this safe space the leader has time to shift the way people think and act before initiating turnaround acts. Kris addresses the issues within the turnaround process that both hinder as well as make possible the major shifts in thinking and acting that are essential for turnaround.

Kris sounds a warning to those contemplating transformation—prepare yourself for survival in the wilderness. So she shares with us ten survival tips that will help a pastor create a safe environment or culture in which transformation is possible without unnecessarily stepping on a time bomb or two. She focuses more on the potential landmines within the transformation process and how to defuse them rather than on the prescriptions for turnaround.

I recommend that you purchase a copy of this book for every person on your turnaround team and enjoy the ride.

Bill Easum
cofounder, Easum, Bandy, Tenny-Brittian
www.easumbandy.com

PREFACE

Today the concept of *transformation* is the buzzword of many congregations and nearly every denomination. (Sure, some use the term *revitalization*, while others object that this presupposes a previous time of vitality.) Books, seminars, workshops, workbooks, tapes, programs, coaches, and consultants glut the market; yet churches are still declining and closing and, in the popular jargon of many, "wandering around in survival mode."

In fact, my original working title for this book was *How to Avoid Congregational Suicide*, after a jarring wake-up call to the dynamic of congregational self-destruction. I had been asked to facilitate the growth of a congregation from an at-best worship attendance of less than one hundred members to three services that would sometimes reach more than two hundred participants in a given week. Our budget grew significantly, our Christian education ministries mushroomed, and the baptistery was being used again with not only youth but also adults. Mission to the community and beyond kept growing. All the indicators were positive.

But after an intentional discernment process, that congregation decided it would rather be small than grow beyond the three hundred in worship they had called me to facilitate. With the change in focus—and not fathoming myself a chaplain or decline pastor—I resigned. Within a year, most of the leaders and new members who had come during my time as pastor were worshiping in other congregations. And the worship attendance, back to one service, had again dropped below one hundred. Within two years after my resignation, worship attendance was at sixty-five, too low to make much ministry and mission possible. Today that church is thinking about merging with another congregation that has been ministering ten miles away, in a totally different neighborhood and setting—their decision resting on economics rather than mission and vision.

This shortening of potential life I call suicide because this small congregation will eventually die out, unable to minister to its wider community or even sustain its own operations. Of course, not every congregation is so intentional about its decline or decision not to grow. By the same token, a pastor can do all the "right" things, even figure out the "right" programs and policies for a congregation, and the church will still not survive the journey of transformation.

The reason: a thin line rests between the transformational journey and suicide. Not everyone likes the metaphor of suicide, mostly out of a genuine respect for those who have seriously engaged the choice to end their lives. After several correspondences with my publisher, I have come to see that what we face—or, perhaps more accurately, ignore—in many of our congregations is a ticking time bomb. Sometimes these bombs are buried in closets with skeletons; sometimes they're masked with tapes of fear or guilt and shame; sometimes they look scarily like folks in our congregations. A congregation desiring to be in transformation mode needs to create safe environments for building trust, defusing ticking time bombs, and holding the transformational journey intact.

When I refer to *transformation*, I am referring to a state of being, not a state—or place—of arrival. It's currently popular for congregations to seek to become "transformed"; but the truth is that we never can be completely transformed nor should we want to be. To be "transformed" connotes that we will again find ourselves in an unchanging mode, a static place. Rather, what I believe congregations are faithfully called to be is *transformational* so that they can encourage, equip, and empower personal, community, and global transformation.

I wish someone had told me that sooner. And I wish someone had offered me a few hints about how to keep ourselves and the congregations we serve on the transformational path. Instead, I've taken the initiative with this book to suggest ten necessary ways for a congregation to identify the ticking time bombs, to defuse them, and to move on into the transformational journey.

Top 10 Ways to Defuse Your Congregational Time Bomb comes out of twenty-five years of experiences as a lay person, pastor, and middle-judicatory executive in transformational churches. I am well steeped in the language and learnings of the church-growth, health, and transformation movements: I've dedicated most of my adulthood, much of my education, and all of my professional life to them. Alas, for every success story I have myriad examples of congregations that still struggle, and I have too many stories of churches that have closed. Since my own personal story of transformation from being a teenage runaway who dropped out of school in eleventh grade is a story rooted in the ministry and mission of the local congregation, my heart continues to be drawn to congregational "success."

This book is grounded in the conviction that we are called to fulfill the "Four Greats": the Great Invitation, the two Great Commandments, and the Great Commission. Though more an undercurrent than an overt focus, the chapters unfold out of these Greats: Chapters 1–6 are intended to help congregations live into the Great Commission and Great Invitation; chapters 7–9 are grounded in the command to love others, and chapter 10 correlates with the command to love God. In the vein of "the first shall be last and the last shall be first," this book ends with the Great Commandment to love God with the whole of our being because, quite frankly, transformation is impossible if it is neither grounded in nor guided by God.

In this same spirit, first and foremost I want to acknowledge God, the Almighty, who created me for work such as this; Jesus, my Sovereign and Savior, who has enabled me to do work such as this; and the Holy Spirit, who has breathed this work into and through me. May the Trinity be glorified through this work.

I also want to thank those who have been affiliated with Bakke Graduate University, where this work was birthed: Gwen Dewey, Lowell Bakke, and John Sharpe—their grace and God-reflectedness have repeatedly motivated and encouraged me along the way; and Dr. Rick Kingham and Dr. Steve Ogne, who have pushed me to understand better the relationships between leadership, congregational health, and the potential for transformation and eventual kingdom multiplication. (Indeed, Steve, it's not about growing a church or denomination; it's about growing the realm of God, thank you.)

I also must thank my colleagues in the Bethany Fellowships: Don Schutt, Kim Gage Ryan, Bob Hill, Gary Straub, and David Shirey, who are models and encouragers par excellence! I would be remiss if I didn't mention Martha Grace Reese, with whom I have had the privilege of journeying for over ten years now: first as a mentor and now as a colleague and friend. I am eternally grateful for your prayers, insights, and the privilege of sharing the journey with you.

And for those who are working with me in the bringing of this book to publication and light: thank you. Thank you, Uli and Kris, for your guidance; your listening, reading, and thoughtful suggestions—your ability to see what I'm trying to say and make it clearer. Kris, thank you for your attention to detail and willingness to "trade horses." Joan, I appreciate your care. And thank you, too, Tim, for taking a chance on this work and its message. I am grateful to you and to The Pilgrim Press.

Finally, I turn to thank my family. As I have mentioned, the first shall be last and the last shall be first. Alas, all too often those God has entrusted to my care—namely my children and husband—have been last. And while I mention them last in this dedication, their love, steadfastness, encouragement, and support remain primary. Thank you, Britt, Shannon, and Kat, for the ways you continually allow me to be your mother in spite of the challenges of being PKs in too many survival-minded churches: you have been, and remain, oases in the deserts and I am proud of each of you. And to you, William, thank you for standing by me in the good times as well as when defusing bombs, when others are taking aim and, yes, even when I'm shooting myself. How can I begin to thank you for holding my hand and my head through the deserted wildernesses, for listening to me cry, complain, kvetch, and curse ad nauseam; and for nearly always being there at *any* hour not only to listen but to process and pray? I remain indebted to you all.

introduction

Many congregations are in survival mode. Mainline congregations—even those who have labored to promote church growth, effectiveness, success, or transformation—will rarely fight this conclusion. But they do want to know: What went wrong?

Some blame the confusion on theological assumptions: Mainliners "aren't supposed to be pushy about our religion," so we cannot necessarily expect our churches to grow. Many think churches should place more emphasis on changing the world through political and social movements than on opening individuals to the change that comes through a personal relationship with God through Jesus Christ. Quite a few of us put more emphasis on congregational growth than on the growth of God's realm. And how we love to debate all this! But all too often these dynamics have become excuses for not living the Great Commandments, Jesus' directives (a) to love God with all our heart, soul, and mind, and (b) to love others as ourselves,[1] and the Great Commission, Jesus' decree that we go out into the world to baptize, teach, and make disciples of all nations.[2]

In turn, the confusion is having a serious effect on congregations. While statistics vary as to how much, the fact remains that mainline denominations are shrinking. A recent research project studying adult baptism (representing adult faith conversion) in mainline congregations that are predominantly Anglo and located north of the Bible belt was able to identify out of a potential thirty thousand congregations fewer than 150 that had baptized more than fifteen adults over a three-year period (an average of five adults per year).[3] While adult baptisms are not the only way individual congregations grow, this statistic means that mainline congregations are subject to the surplus or deficiency of births to deaths.

The first sign of congregational decline that is typically noticed is financial. It may be that a congregation needs at least one hundred members to support a full-time pastor, yet the fact is that only half the congregations in the United States number more than seventy-five participants on a "regular" weekend. This average reflects typical urban attendance of one hundred, and typical rural attendance of fewer than fifty congregants.[4] Although many of these smaller congregations strive to maintain a full-time pastorate, it is increasingly difficult, if not impossible, for pastors to responsibly live on what a hundred-member congregation can afford to pay, let alone a fifty-member congregation.

But clergy salaries aren't the only line items we are having trouble affording. We also juggle building maintenance, programming, mission, and denominational support. Many congregations have come to equate success and effectiveness with finishing the fiscal year in the black rather than in the red.

And we are seeing congregations close. Tom Clegg and Warren Bird tell us that three times as many churches in America are closing (3,750) as are opening (1,300) each year. Bill Easum has predicted that 75 percent of mainline churches will close over the next twenty-five or so years. I've heard it said that 33 percent of the mainline churches in existence in 2000 will no longer be regularly worshiping in 2010. Lyle Schaller puts a figure to those percentages, proposing that number to be somewhere between one hundred thousand and one hundred fifty thousand congregations.[5]

Understandably, in the midst of such congregational decline, the pressure for effective growth and success is heightened. Congregational pastors (or their designees) are required by mainline denominations to submit statistical information at least once a year. We know that these reports are often mistakenly entered or, worse, embellished in the areas of baptism, membership, and worship attendance; and pastors commonly will do a "push" for baptisms toward the close of the year so that they can demonstrate "growth," or, at the very least, the appearance of near maintenance. Even denominational bodies embellish their numbers, counting congregations that have not reported in as many as five years or more.

I do not mean to paint a picture of congregations, pastors, or judicatory leaders as misleading, perfunctory, detached, or removed from their spiritual roots. Alas, we *can* easily succumb to the pressure of church growth and success, particularly as we see more and more congregations and judicatories searching and reaching for the newest program, the newest book, the newest promise of visible, fast results and solutions to our latest emergencies.

But lest we jump too quickly into talking about solutions, let us speak once again about the dynamic of survival. In his article "The Attitude of Survival," Chris Conway offers that

> survival is the art of surviving beyond any event. To survive means to remain alive, to live. Survival is taking any given circumstance, accepting it, and trying to improve it, while sustaining your life until you can get out of the situation.

Chris adds that survival depends on our ability to endure stress in emergency situations.[6]

Many (some would say *most*) congregations are facing at least one emergency situation: financial crises, building matters (that is, maintenance or mortgage mishaps), worship attendance, member retention, or how to sustain programming.

You can read about them regularly in church newsletters, often with vivid details. Month after month too many churches are transferring money from their endowment funds and savings to their checking accounts to cover operating expenses. This is an emergency situation. At least once a year you can read the repeated reminders for folks to get their stewardship pledges in. This is an emergency situation. You can read the pleas of exasperated committee chairs trying to "attract" people to participate in their particular ministry with the very real threat that they may not be able to do "such-and-such" because not enough folks are supporting it. This is an emergency situation. In still other newsletters you will read of the same few individuals wearing many hats in order to maintain or save ministries that frankly have no sustainable momentum. This is an emergency situation. You can read about the programs cancelled or "postponed" for lack of participation. This is an emergency situation. You can see pastors pouring out their hearts in their pastor's columns about how attendance has been declining and everyone needs to bring a friend on a given Sunday. And while "Bring a Friend Sunday" can be a viable evangelism option, pastor-poured guilt is not. Indeed, this is an emergency situation.

And as in all emergency situations, there is the potential to slip into survival mode, to do whatever it will take to make it through—or at least to think we can do whatever it takes.

Now, hold that thought while we consider another type of situation that causes me to talk about survival.

Mainline denominations have been spending a lot of time and energy, if not dollars, on this subject of congregational transformation, or revitalization. Several years ago, while I was serving as an associate regional minister, folks in denominational judicatory work were increasingly using the word "transformation" rather than "revitalization" because we had to admit that some of our congregations had never really been "vital."

One of the congregations I pastored has a file at the regional office that is stuffed with complaints reaching back over forty years, some about the congregation and others about the pastors. Another congregation I served had asked every pastor in its forty-eight-year history to leave— with the exception of its first and myself. Another congregation I have known and loved recently said good-bye to its third pastor (not including the two interims) in nine years.

Surely you have such stories, too. A recent study of pastors who have left congregational ministry revealed that the most common reasons for leaving were (1) to pursue specialized ministry and (2) frustrations from dealing with conflict.[7] And while 27 percent of those pastors left specifically because of conflict in the congregation, 39 percent of *all* the studied ex-pastors noted the presence of major church conflict within the congregations they left. Conflict is necessary and indeed healthy. But the fact is that much congregational conflict is handled, or not, in unhealthy ways, to the detriment of pastors, laity, and churches. And the truth is that many such congregations have not been healthy for a very long time.

Now, we add to that mix this process called transformation. A growing mass of literature analyzes transformation: how the process works, how to effect it, the elements found in transformed congregations, and more. A study of the elements identified as critical for transformational congregations reveals ten key "ingredients"—what in this book I call the Ten Ways:

1. A commitment to faith that is solid, active, and alive and opportunities to discover, nurture, and grow that faith.

2. A variety of opportunities to engage in mission beyond the church's doors.

3. Organizational structures that are streamlined to release and multiply, rather than impede, ministry.

4. Worship that is relevant to the congregation and those they are trying to reach.

5. Core leadership that empowers others to become disciples who help others become Christians and disciples to still others.

6. Intentional lay training and deployment.

7. Solid stewardship that allows for adequate, responsible financing.

8. Ministry that is based on the discovery and sharing of people's spiritual gifts.

9. Small groups that are relevant and create deep, transparent, spiritual friendships.

10. A policy or "system" that is permission-giving, freeing people to use their gifts and passions within and beyond the context of the congregation as long as their ministries are within the scope of the congregation's mission, vision, and values.[8]

Maybe you recognize some or all of these ingredients in your congregation, but more than likely you do not. And *that* is what the process of transformation is about: moving us from where we are to implementing policies, structures, and practices that reflect these ingredients, or ones similar to them. But we do not engage this process for the sake of process alone. We engage it so that our congregations can be places where lives and even the world are being transformed.

These shifts in thinking, doing, and being are not easy, nor can they easily be "charted." We can, however, predict a number of challenges and reactions along the way, Yet our predictions do not change the facts of what people are thinking or feeling and how they may be reacting or acting out.

Quite honestly, the transformational journey between "where we are" (let alone "where we have been") and "where we are going" is fraught with some very scary and desolate places and there are times it seems as though you will find an improvised explosive device (IED) at every turn. Attendance doesn't grow as quickly as we anticipate, the income is declining, long-time members are threatening to leave or, worse yet, have already begun exiting. Like the Israelites wandering around in the desert for forty years, we anticipate the promised landing of more people in our pews and more secure financing but we aren't sure we can count on it. After a while, most of us can't even envision it. Yet this wilderness looks and feels and actually is quite hostile: it is marked at times by hotter than hot tempers and plenty of cold shoulders and icy stares. It is fraught with problems we can't fix and new challenges that appear on a regular basis, often at the most inconvenient times. Frustration, anxiety, anger, fear, and panic regularly descend like plagues. When congregations are fortunate to experience a "lull" between crises, boredom is likely to set in and set off another round of disgruntlement. Depression is not uncommon nor is guilt, particularly among the leadership, who wonder why on earth they ever set off on this "adventure." People get tired to the point of fatigue; loneliness sets in as our friends abandon and avoid us; and there is talk of and even unconscious, self-sabotaging attempts at giving up. We wonder if it's worth the danger to our health, wealth, and well-being.

Transformation is a long journey that often seems more arduous than adventuresome. It often begs the question: How long are we going to be able to support and sustain the promised land path? There are some things we can do to become better equipped to continue the journey.

Before we get to them, understand this: many of our congregations ostensibly engaging "transformation" are actually flirting with ticking time bombs and thus with suicide. Yes, really.

Think about it: some of the commonly identified natural responses to wilderness survival situations are: fear, anxiety, anger, frustration, loneliness, boredom, guilt, and depression. Notice any parallels with the transformational wanderings of congregations? Often these factors lead to thoughts of suicide. Indeed, much of the wilderness survival literature talks about the importance of keeping a positive attitude if one is going to survive an emergency situation. And we have to think clearly, practically, and deliberately.

There is more good news. First, our suicidal leanings can be averted and can become points for healing. In fact, much of what many of us are doing in our congregations is more like shooting ourselves in the foot rather than in the head and we can recover from our wounds. To come back to our time bomb metaphor: we need to be careful because so many of us have played with exploding bombs for so long that our health and ability to wander transformationally are critically impaired and in question.

Defusing bombs is dangerous and delicate work that must be engaged in safe and secure places. In *Leadership on the Line,* Ron Heifetz and Marty Linsky talk about the need for *holding environments,* "space formed by a network of relationships within which people can tackle tough, sometimes divisive questions without flying apart." Such holding environments provide "structural, procedural, or virtual boundaries [within which] people feel safe enough to address problems that are difficult, not only because they strain ingenuity, but also because they strain relationships." Holding environments look different in different places, but they include contexts such as a community's shared language and common history, deep trust in the institution, and clear sets of rules and processes. Heifetz and Linsky warn, "The design of the holding environment . . . is a major strategic challenge—it must be sound, or else you risk the success of the change effort."9

Too many of our congregations in survival mode have compromised holding capacities and, given the nature of their wilderness wanderings, are themselves hostile environments rather than safe ones conducive to the transformation we so desperately need and seek. As a wandering wilderness people, we have lost our common history, and language means little for people whose common patterns of conversation include little more than hello-how-are-you exchanges on Sunday morning. The rules and processes on which we have relied are not always the healthiest (such as the post–board meeting parking lot gatherings). In such situations trust has been eroding for a while; and whom can we trust anyway? Many of us aren't even sure we can trust God.

Wilderness survival experts remind us that there are a number of ways we can prepare ourselves for survival situations. Good common sense dictates that those who anticipate going into the wilderness need to prepare for possible survival situations. Preparations commonly mentioned include getting to know ourselves and how we react under pressure, anticipating our fears, becoming realistic about the situations in which we may find ourselves, adopting positive attitudes, reminding ourselves of what can be at stake (such as our lives and the lives of those who depend on us), training in survival skills, and stress management techniques.[10] Likewise, if we are anticipating or already engaging congregational transformation, we need to be as prepared as possible for the hostile wilderness environment and for the threats to our survival along the way. Do we have holding environments in place that will keep us together while we meet the new challenges?

Another piece of good news is that we can create or hone some relatively simple holding environments; indeed, many are already found in our congregations. These will not only prepare us to engage transformation; they will help to hold the journey while we defuse the time bombs we find along the way.

Top 10 Ways to Defuse Your Congregational Time Bomb is a book of survival tips for those wandering the wilderness of transformation. What we are talking about are tips that, when practiced, can create environments for holding transformation. You may find that your congregation is already practicing some of these, and you will no doubt notice that others are missing from your repertoire. The better prepared we are for wilderness wandering survival, the more likely we are to lay down our weapons and prevent any further attempts at destruction. And, of course, the more environments for holding transformation we have, the better.

Before we move ahead, let me quickly note that I hold a number of biases; the most germane for this context are the following:

- I believe God calls the church to be faithful in its mission to continually invite, equip, empower, and encourage people to love God and others with the whole of their very beings. How that works out is as individual as are congregations and the people who find themselves gathered together.

- I also believe that true, radical, and sustainable change in people's lives and in the world as a whole (socially, economically, politically, etc.) will come only when every person in every place not only knows God through Jesus Christ and the Holy Spirit but also lives in an active, vital relationship with God.

Notes

1. See Matthew 22:34–40 and Mark 12:28–31.

2. See Matthew 28:16–20.

3. The Mainline Evangelism Research Project was funded by the Lilly Endowment and conducted by GraceNet through the Office of the General Minister and President of the Christian Church (Disciples of Christ). See *Unbinding the Gospel: Real Life Evangelism* by Martha Grace Reece, the president of GraceNet and director of the project (St. Louis, MO: Chalice Press, 2006).

4. Nancy T. Ammerman, *Doing Good in American Communities: Congregations and Service Organizations Working Together* (Hartford, CT: Hartford Institute for Religion Research, 2005).

5. Tom Clegg and Warren Bird, *Lost in America: How You and Your Church Can Impact the World Next Door* (Loveland, CO: Group Publishing, 2001), 30. Lyle Schaller, *Tattered Trust: Is There Hope for Your Denomination?* (Nashville: Abingdon Press, 1996), 26.

6. Chris Conway, "The Attitude Of Survival," 1999, http://www.geocities.com/Yosemite/Falls/9200/survival_attitude.html.

7. Dean R. Hoge and Jacqueline E. Wenger, *Pastors in Transition: Why Clergy Leave Local Church Ministry* (Grand Rapids: William B. Eerdmans, 2005), 97.

8. J. Kristina Tenny-Brittian, "Ingredients of a Growing Church," unpublished paper.

9. Ronald Heifetz and Marty Linsky, *Leadership on the Line: Staying Alive through the Dangers of Leading* (Boston: Harvard Business School Press, 2002), 102–3.

10. Wilderness Survival, "Preparing Yourself," http://www.wilderness-survival.net/mind-3.php.

1

FACE YOUR MONEY FEARS

Perhaps you're thinking, "Whew-HOO! She knows exactly what we need: let's start with the money. After all, that's what we're lacking." I know that in many of our churches the financial situation is dire, and that depleted cash reserves and declining income are two of the greatest motivators for engaging transformation. But money is not the *source* of transformation, although it is too often foremost on our minds. I place it here first only because I want us to address it and move forward.

APPROACHING MATTERS OF MONEY

I'll say it again: Money is not the *source* of transformation. Indeed, lack of sufficient finances is not *the* problem for any of us; it is an *effect* of the problem. I have heard it said for many years that lack of finances is not a matter of money but a matter of faith, and I have come to find that this is true. Church consultant Tom Bandy points out that property, outward communication (such as advertising and marketing), and finances are the three subsystems churches think "will most powerfully leverage their church into a healthy future." So it is understandable that because it looms so large for many of us, we want to start with the matter of money and then base everything else we plan and do—or can't do—around it. But Tom cautions that churches can have "no idea what to do about" property, communication, and finances unless they first address other systems in the congregation.[1]

There are a number of basic generational differences by which some (though by no means all) of us understand money, faith, and financial matters in the church. People who have come through the Great Depression are more likely to be savers and keepers of "rainy day" funds. The buildings and endowed funds my generation (late-baby-boomer) is inheriting must be credited very much to that Depression era generation: you have tended to be generously conservative in your spending and genuinely generous in preparing for the future. You tend not to purchase anything until you can pay for it in full, avoiding time payments, or buying on credit, as much as possible. You know the joy of burning mortgages and have little desire to take on new debt in your own personal lives or in the life of the church.

Beyond the generational perspective, though, our approaches to finances in the church also reflect our own approaches to our personal finances. Those of us "at the top of our game" who are adeptly juggling debt and are holding out for resources yet to come are often much more open to investing and "doing whatever it takes" to ensure "the future." Some would call this a perspective of *abundance*: there is a trust that there will nearly always be more than enough resources at our disposal to meet our needs.

Conversely, many of us who are living into fixed incomes are as cautious as possible about assuming new debt, so we tend to experience a greater resistance to debt assumption; we tend to put more emphasis on taking care of what we have and resist taking on additional financial responsibilities. While a highly responsible way of approaching money, some (with Walter Brueggemann) might call this perspective one of *scarcity*: we are more concerned about what is not—and may not—be available than we are with what resources may be there in the future.

Those of us who have been good stewards, taking care of what God has provided, are more like managers of what has been given. Our emphasis tends to be more on *what has been given* than *what is yet to be given*. This is a "past-oriented" perspective, fixed on what we can know for sure, rather than a "future-oriented" perspective, which can be a little unsure and a lot unsettling. After all, it is generally easier to try to control the known rather than trust in the unknown. Folks who live in abundance tend to be bigger risk takers than those who have lived, or live, with a sense of scarcity.

Those of us who have encountered loss may well know scarcity. Those who live within the paradigm of scarcity tend to be cautious about what we have, often wanting to hold on to it closely, even to the point of controlling as much as we can around us. Perhaps we have tried to control people, issues, situations, and finances so we don't lose them or use them up. But the reality is, the control we *think* we are exerting can actually come to control us! We can find ourselves immobilized, hesitant to make a decision about this or that, exerting a level of caution that is based on our discomfort with risking or losing anything. We come to live out of fear of scarcity rather than living by what we know in our spirit: that God is a God of abundance and wants to provide for us "the desires of our hearts!"

THE DESIRES OF OUR HEARTS

Now, "desires of our hearts" may sound like an odd concept to some of us. I had an administrative assistant a few years back who seemed to delight in reminding our staff that "God wants to give you the desires of your heart." I would listen, but her words did not hit home until a couple of years ago when I realized a lot of the people with whom I was working in the church were seriously lacking hope. I began to ask them about their dreams and desires. They could often tell me about unfulfilled and broken dreams and desires, but were understandably reticent—even unable—to talk about what they would like for themselves. One day I blurted out to someone in my office, "How can God give you the desires of your heart if you're not willing to name those desires?" After agreeing that God gives without our asking, I asked, "Then how will you know that God has given you the desire of your heart if you are afraid to admit to it? And how will you glorify God by telling others what [God] has done for you if you haven't claimed it up front?²

I figured I had better do a little scripture search to make sure my strange-sounding comments about God wanting to give us the desires of

13

our hearts make biblical sense! Passages from the Psalms were particular fruitful: Psalm 20:4; Psalm 21:2; and Psalm 37:4, to name just a few.[3]

There's a danger in this, isn't there? After all, what happens when the desires of our hearts are greedy or not particularly kind or positive? And what happens when those desires fly in the face of God's desires? First let me say that we are not talking about a "health and wealth gospel" here: this is not about everyone getting rich or having more and bigger toys than anyone else. We are also not talking about the desires of our hearts being a vehicle for getting rid of troublesome people in our lives.

Instead, it's about our hearts being aligned with God's heart. We are meant to say at the end of our prayers, as we do in the prayer Jesus taught the disciples, "Your will be done, God." We can ask and expect God to answer, but we need to be open to how *God* is going to answer. In the prophet Isaiah (26:8 NIV) we read, "Lord, walking in the way of your laws, we wait for you; your name and renown are the desire of our hearts."

In short, the desire of our heart is meant to be for God and God's renown. I love the part of the Prayer of Confession in the Episcopalian *Book of Common Prayer* that asks God for forgiveness so that we may delight in God's will and walk in God's ways, to the glory of God's name.[4]

MONEY, DESIRE, AND STEWARDSHIP

Stewardship is ultimately about delighting in *God's* will and desiring to walk in *God's* ways—but we will have more to say about that later. For now, let me suggest that when our churches are striving to (a) be the kind of churches God created us to be and (b) do the things God wants us to do, God will make sure we have what we need *as long as we get out of God's way and stop controlling the money.* Should we ask questions? Yes! Be careful? Definitely! Exert control? No . . . because ultimately those things we try to control end up controlling us!

But there is more to stewardship than managing resources. Stewardship is not a once-a-year program. What if we took a different approach and started with the belief that the finances of the church are not ours; they are God's? Beyond that, our finances are not ours: they, too, belong to God. Throughout the Bible we see echoed the words of

14

the writer of Psalm 24 in the Older Testament of the Bible, who put it this way:

> The earth is the Lord's, and all that is in it, the world, and those who live in it; for [God] founded it on the seas, and established it on the rivers." (Psalm 24:1–2)

We are all stewards—the keepers of that which has been entrusted to us—but that which has been entrusted to us comprises not only the congregation's property, endowment funds, programs, and parishioners; it includes *everything* for which we are ultimately responsible in our lives, namely, our time, talent, and treasure. If, indeed, all that we have and all that we own is God's, we have a responsibility to hold it out for God to use as God has need and desire. With that comes a sense that God is in charge and that God will provide as we have need.

Ironically, several annual stewardship campaign resources in recent years have been based on this concept of stewardship. To be sure, it is not easy to practice. Biblical stewardship challenges us to tithe (that is, to give 10 percent of our income, including interest earned and lottery monies won) or to follow the Newer Testament's example of "giving it all."[5]

There is not enough room in this chapter to go more deeply into the topic of tithing and stewardship. Suffice it to say that too many of us in the church have either been sold a faulty bill of goods when it comes to stewardship or have neglected to take seriously God's charge to be good stewards. This is a critical point in the premise that lack of funding comes down to "lack of faith."

On one hand, stewardship is a traditional spiritual discipline: we practice it because "the Bible tells us so." But it is not some banal exercise we engage in out of obedience. Stewardship is an invaluable teacher; through it, we learn to trust God's provision for us—fostering a level of trust that is rooted in our cores, not our heads. To give away 10 percent of our income can be a far stretch for most of us, but stories abound about the difference this discipline makes to people who practice it. Tithers know how God can provide from seemingly "out of nowhere" and can multiply what they figured would never be enough. They tend to have depths of trust and hope that many of us have never considered, let alone lived out.

15

On the other hand, stewardship moves us past obedience to desire. I must confess I am not the most cheerful of givers; my husband keeps the checkbook and makes sure our collective tithe now gets paid up front. When it has depended on me, I have generally found some excuse not to write the check, even though we had sufficient funds. Even so, I am grateful for the practice of tithing (and giving beyond) because there have been quite a few months when I have had to rely on God to get us through to the end.

At the outset, tithing seems to increase the real threat of not having sufficient funds to get through a week, let alone a month or year. But most tithers will tell you that as long as they have been *responsible* with what they have, they have had sufficient provisions. Many even share stories of how they have been surprised in ways beyond their imaginations: financial gifts they never suspected, neighbors wanting to share from the bounty of their gardens, an opportunity to make a few extra dollars, a rebate on a power bill. My family has experienced all these, and more, in our lives. As I like to tell folks, "This stuff works!" And that is what motivates my desire: to give back to God a portion of what God has given to me, meager as it may be, in an effort to thank God and help others come to know that kind of love and work in their lives.

God multiplies the time, talent, treasure, and testimony we give to the church by everyone else's to increase the church's witness into the world. Of course, that depends on others practicing stewardship as we are talking about it here. When our churches raise and support good stewards who are tithing, or even giving in proportion to their incomes, we will experience far fewer "financial crises" in our congregations. There will, no doubt, always be a need for more money because the demands of ministry cost a lot, but we will be able to move away from the crisis mentality that plagues too many of our congregations. The crisis that prevents this all from happening, though, *is* one of faith: insufficient faith to trust God to provide either for ourselves or for the ministries God desires.

Now, let's look at this through another dynamic. As more people in the church grow in the spiritual discipline of giving, the church grows in its ability to trust. Of course, a problem arises when "the folks in the pews" are growing spiritually and the leaders are not. This is a leadership issue, and it has caused problems for more than one church. The trick is to get a commitment from your leadership, perhaps challenging them to engage in this as an "experiment" they can then model and share with the congregation. I like to take the approach, "Who knows!?! What have we got to lose?" For when it comes to money, we have everything to gain!

Adequate money comes through adequate continual stewardship training and support, not through stewardship campaigns that are waged once or twice a year or through pleas from the pulpit. As a discipline, stewardship is a way of living for individuals *and* for churches. A lot of us—particularly those of us in mainline churches—do not like that. I once had a pastor in our denomination lodge a complaint against me with the judicatory office because he felt my teaching and expectation of tithing was "too fundamentalist," counter to mainline thought. It is certainly fundamental in the sense of being basic and grounded. But the complaint remains erroneous: a number of growing churches are teaching and practicing tithing, including mainline churches. Do not be afraid of it.

FACING OUR MONEY FEARS

This brings us to one of the greatest challenges we face about money: *fear*. Many of our congregations are experiencing an inordinate amount of stress about money, so much so that many of us are being blindsided by our anxiety (or that of others); and some of us have escalated into sheer panic marked by fully unfounded fears. Often board meetings will stall at the finance report, which is by far the most time-consuming portion of many meetings. Board members quickly forget (if they even heard) the good things ministry leaders report as soon as someone asks "How much did that cost us?" or "Can we afford that?" Boards are nipping in the bud proposed and potentially vital ministries and programs for "lack of funding."

Somehow boards and congregations are able to mirror and magnify the fear and panic of a few people, often the controlling types, or controllers. Our reticence to talk about giving, and to be up-front about giving, exacerbates this issue. In many churches, few people know who gives what, and usually the pastor is not one of those people. While there is much to be said about confidentiality, we are seeing an increasing number of churches that keep their pastor "in the loop": perhaps not with exact dollar figures but with a sense of where people are with their stewardship. A sudden drop in giving has been known to signal a turn for the worse in one's financial condition. It can also note a change in one's spiritual condition.

As often happens in transformational settings, there was a congregation in a wealthy community in which three couples threatened to stop "paying" on the pledges they had made for the year; in fact, one threatened, "I'm going to stop paying on my tithe." Of course, these threats were made loudly and strategically and the executive committee sprang into action, discussing how to avert a "crisis." They thought to check with the finance secretary to see how much of the church's funding was at risk. They soon learned that the sum total of the three couples' threatened withholdings amounted to less than a whopping $3,000.

That may be a lot for your church, but this was a potentially wealthy congregation. There were people in the congregation on public assistance who were actually giving almost as much as the approximately $1,000 per couple these three couples were threatening to withhold. Obviously, none of the couples was tithing, or giving proportionately, and their pledges amounted to little when considered within the larger context of the budget. Beyond that, the members of the executive committee could have covered those lost pledges with an additional gift of sixty dollars per month. To their credit, the executive committee did not pander to the threats and the money was never missed. We mustn't be foolhardy with our money, but neither can we allow money to be wielded as an object of control.

How can we find ways to address our fears and avert the panic? Some congregations have moved the finance report closer to the end of their board meetings—after they have considered all the other reports and proposed ministries, but before they consider any new business—so that they have a better chance to create some momentum and make sound business decisions out of possibility rather than negativity and gloom. Some congregations are beginning to anticipate the questions of cost by talking about return: the number of "new" people who were reached or served, or how the congregation furthered its stated mission or purpose.

FACING OTHER MONEY CHALLENGES

Besides fear, we still have a few other challenges to overcome. Loren Mead has written that churches are misappropriating funds, not with malice aforethought but with a disconnection from the intentions of the givers. He explains:

> Those who give to their congregations do so for a variety of motives and in a variety of styles—from those who "pay their dues" to those who want to "make an impression" to those who give in simple gratitude to God. But there is an implicit contract in all cases that the resources will be used to support the purposes and concerns of the religious community. People who give to churches expect that the money will be used for the purposes— the mission—of that church. Most people are prepared to trust their leaders and give some latitude in how the funds are spent. They know that it may be important to support some things they are not enthusiastic about. They expect that their money will be used to make a difference in something important.

He asserts that over the "past few generations a gap has grown between what 'mission' means to the spenders of the money and the givers of the money."[6] In one congregation this "gap" was manifested when the trustees refused to release the funds needed to repair the leaking baptistery. The congregation's long-timers believed it wasn't used enough to warrant the expense, while the younger parents and youth found the leak tragic. It was a soon-to-be Eagle Scout's proposed project that solved the problem.

In another congregation, an outcry arose from a handful of the congregation's long-timers when the executive committee recommended hiring a second full-time staff pastor in the midst of the financial campaign. This church had a history of first developing their budget and then providing for it through the annual stewardship campaign. Because of circumstances—and opportunity—beyond the executive team's control, the request to add a new staff member came to the board two weeks into the campaign, a month after the proposed budget had been mailed to the congregation and after some of the older, loyal folks had already pledged their support for the proposed budget.

To say many of the long-timers serving on the board were unhappy about the prospect that some of their money might support what they perceived as an excessive expenditure would be an understatement; they were indignant. Word spread like wildfire. Emergency meetings were held. We could frame this as a lack of understanding or a communication breakdown or a manifestation of the pervasive lack of trust between key long-timers and leadership; but it also serves as an example of perceived misappropriation and it proved to be one of the largest roadblocks to transformation in that congregation.

But this sense of fund misappropriation is not only about a lack of understanding on the part of long-time members; it can be found among newer members as well. Sometimes newer members can misunderstand the need to send money to support the denomination, and explanations do not always dispel the frustration of those who would rather spend more in local outreach. New folks who are without the history of signing a second mortgage on their own home to raise building funds or who are void of mortgage burning memories are apt to consider the exorbitant amounts of money budgeted and spent on the repair of a dying building that has outgrown (or ingrown?) its purpose to be bad stewardship.

The way we receive money can also present a challenge for us today. Most congregations still receive money via check and cash, but a lot of our younger people carry neither cash nor checks; they carry debit and credit cards. They don't have much need for cash, keeping track of expenditures by way of on-line check-ins with their bank and credit card accounts (the latter for which they get airline mileage).

There are a lot of congregations left empty-handed because they have not made provisions for giving through the use of debit cards or automatic deductions. A number of congregations retain stock brokers so that they can annually receive income from stock transfers and leverage those to their benefit. Some congregations are now accepting credit cards, but I am reticent to advocate for them here because credit card debt is a serious problem for too many of us and I cannot recommend encouraging it. Congregations can also help their folks to give by providing no-nonsense training in healthy spending and debt reduction, thus allowing people to lower their debt and be able to more realistically live into stewardship practices like tithing.

All these suggestions, however, may not change the fact that your congregation is finding itself with seriously compromised funding and no fast solutions as to how to increase it and fund your way out of the wilderness.

FINDING THE FUNDS FOR SURVIVAL

When the funds our congregations need are nowhere to be found, we have to be creative with what we have. A congregation I served was fortunate to have as a member a woman studying for the ministry whose passion was worship and spiritual growth. With a little research, the member found a potential grant that would allow the congregation to pay a portion of a salary for her while she employed her gifts—one of the church's values—and furthered the congregation's mission and vision. It took several months, but the grant was awarded, and she was able to stay at the church rather than have to "go find a job" somewhere else. She also started an alternative worship service that reached people the congregation had not been able to reach.

Recently I called the pastor of a new church and found him at the library researching grants that would allow his church to fund their signature ministry until it is self-supporting. Other churches are already funding their ministries through the ministries themselves, but their ideas of ministry may not look like many of ours. Some are running pizza parlors and even bars so their members have places to invite their unchurched friends and where they can meet other unchurched folks in their area who come in to patronize their businesses. You might try giving office space to a psychologist who can offer counseling to your members on a sliding-fee scale while building his or her practice. Both of you win: the psychologist gets free office space and potential clients; you get a counseling ministry (the psychologist covers the liability insurance not covered under your own policy). The point is to be creative.

Of course, this can play out different ways. Hence, the following story of two congregations. There is a congregation that sits on a piece of residential land that developers would like to buy for upwards of one million dollars. The church board had before them the three-year portion of a transformational proposal that would necessitate an estimated $100,000 over the projected income for the next three years, with the conservative intention that the congregation would be financially self-sufficient by the end of three years.

The executives brought the proposal to the board with several ideas about how they might fund the $100,000 shortfall, soliciting additional suggestions from the board. One of the suggestions was to sell a small portion of the property they never use, a lot at the back of their land that would compromise neither the integrity nor aesthetics of the property. Several of the people present heard little else than "sell property" and an outcry rippled into a portion of the congregation. Follow-up focus groups were held and all members were personally invited to attend a group to learn more about the proposed three-year process, to gather their thoughts and ideas, and to allow them to express their concerns. Unfortunately these follow-up meetings led to key leaders making unendorsed promises like "I guarantee we will never sell the property."

In the end, it became clear that congregation had a seriously compromised financial environment for holding their much-need transformation. The majority of members did not practice the discipline of stewardship and they were insufficiently prepared to endure the financial rigors of the transformational wilderness. Their anxiety, fear, and panic grew to control their capacity to process and think into the future.

Then there is the story of another congregation in the same denomination and not too far away who found themselves without a music minister. This congregation had been wandering in its own transformational wilderness for some time and it lived with the reality of diminished, inadequate funding. As they considered hiring a new music "person" (because, surely, they could never afford a "minister"), they received an application from an ordained minister with a heart for hope, worship, and transition. This pastor shared a vision for what worship might look like in their setting, but that came with two stark realities: (1) to give the emerging worship ministry the energy and time it would necessitate, the music minister would need a salary that would keep him from having to take on a third job; and (2) the diminished talent pool in the congregation did not provide the talent needed for the kind of worship they were envisioning, so there would be the need to hire a vocalist and possible back-up musicians.

The congregation considered and reconsidered its options. There were no reserves, particularly not for a commitment like this. Now some will question the potential of pinning one's transformational hopes on a worship service, but that is what that congregation chose to do; they only needed to figure out how to fund it. Someone suggested they might sell a piece of their property, which they came to do. Today that congregation has a minister of music and a growing worship team that is working to reach people who do not have a relationship with God.

And the other congregation? A year after resolving not to sell a portion of their property, they were entertaining the prospect of selling the entirety of it.

Be creative when facing financial challenges. Money is one of the key stressors threatening our survival and abilities to engage transformation, and it is not because there is not enough. Our fears are frustrating our abilities to think, process, and discern clearly. A lot of congregations spend a lot of time talking about how much they do not have rather than trying to figure out how much they do have . . . and how to have more. As such, we often less than enthusiastically invest in money pits rather than in trying to grow money trees.

I am reminded of God's provision for the Israelites when they left Egypt:

> Now the Lord had said to Moses . . . "Tell the people that men and women alike are to ask their neighbors for articles of silver and gold." (The Lord made the Egyptians favorably disposed toward the people, and Moses himself was highly regarded in Egypt by Pharaoh's officials and by the people.) (Exod. 11:1–3 NIV)

Who would have ever imagined such riches for slaves, for people about to go out and wander around in the wilderness for forty years? Exactly! We cannot begin to imagine!

I continue to be surprised by how many churches have tens of thousands of dollars (even hundreds of thousands of dollars) in savings yet cannot move past their money fears. And then there are those who now have less than $10,000 in the bank and continue monthly to move money from their savings to their operating accounts. There is a difference between infusing our budgets and investing in our budgets. We are guilty of infusion when we siphon money from savings to operating in an effort to stop the slow bleeds that are sapping our financial security. Infusions lead to the removal of money, not the moving of money as we'd like to believe, because there is no plan for how we will stop the bleeding. Investing, however, comes with a plan: we know we may have to use an additional $10,000 for the next five years to afford the pastor or program or consultant that will work with us to find the slow bleeds and help us to heal and become strong and healthy. It may cost $50,000 or more before we begin to see a return on our investment (and it must be engaged with a clear plan for evaluation); but I have watched countless congregations infuse $50,000 and more over the course of five to ten years without *any* return, without any change or growth, numerical or otherwise.

Over and over again our financial fears and anxieties control and compromise our abilities to consider investing in rather than infusing our budgets. Can you imagine choosing between defusing a time bomb and doing whatever it will take to live fully into the future? That's exactly the choice many of us face, and yet many of us will still choose the time bomb over our future, God's future for us. Remember, time bombs can tick slowly and quietly, but they tick nonetheless. Defusing a time bomb calls for direct and decisive action and allows for few mistakes. Defuse your money fears up front so they won't blow up in your face later!

Notes

1. Tom Bandy (consultant and partner in Easum, Bandy & Associates) in discussion with author, April 2005.

2. Proverbs 16:3 tells us, "Commit your work to the Lord, and your plans will be established."

3. See also Psalm 145:16, 19.

4. *Book of Common Prayer and Administration of the Sacraments and Other Rites and Ceremonies of the Church* (New York: Seabury Press, 1979), 79, adapted.

5. Remember that tithing is an Older Testament concept. It opens the door to offer the Newer Testament option of "giving it all." For more, see Matthew 19:16–26 and Acts 4:32–35.

6. Loren Mead, *Transforming Congregations for the Future* (Herndon, VA: Alban Institute, 1994), 87–88.

2

T AKE W HAT Y OU N EED

A S TREAK OF I NDEPENDENCE

When my husband and I were preparing to move with our three youngest children half-way across the continent to pursue mission in the Pacific Northwest, the acting regional minister there warned us that the white caps on the Cascade Mountains were actually the church membership papers of those moving out there from the East. His comments were well-grounded and actually echoed the observation of E. J. Klemme of the Washington State Normal School, who noted in 1914 that folks relocating to the Pacific Northwest ceased to be the faithful church attenders they once were in the East:

> The ascent of the Great Divide seemed too steep for church letters. The air of the Northwest seemed too rare for prayer. We have hurried forth to conquer the wilderness, but we have been conquered by it.[1]

Indeed, Pacific Northwesterners are quite the independent lot.

But Northwesterners are not alone. We Christians—particularly mainliners—tend to be quite independent as well . . . and we are guilty of a certain amount of elitism. Indeed, when considering alternative methods for doing and being church, we are often quick to dismiss those that are not rooted in the mainline, and with that we risk losing a foot or two.

I remember sitting next to the spouse of a denominational leader during dinner several years ago. The *Prayer of Jabez*[2] was rising on the best seller lists, and someone mentioned the book. The conversation caught my attention because one of my parishioners had given me a copy of it to read, and I was planning to draw on its current popularity to use it as a jumping-off point for a series of upcoming sermons. I listened intently as several folks, including the leader and the spouse, began to dismiss the book as yet another "abundance gospel, health-and-welfare" deal threatening to mislead people. I had not remembered reading that message into the book, so I decided to listen a little more closely, wondering if I had entirely overlooked something to which I should have been better attuned.

As the next hour passed, it became clearer that few of those registering their opinions had actually read the book. I found an opportunity to quietly ask if the denominational leader or spouse had read it; neither had. The question began to move down the table: except for me, no one at the table had read the book, although everyone had a less than tasteful view of it. It turned out that the problem my table company had with the book was that it did not come from a mainline author and yet was gaining momentum on the best-seller list. We were suspicious and wanting to be careful to do what we could do to prevent "bad theology" from infiltrating the minds of our sheep.

I can recount similar conversations since then, many of them about Rick Warren's *The Purpose Driven Life*[3] and the Forty Days of Purpose program. Most of the time, the conversationalists had never read the book; fewer had taken the time to explore the whole of the program. Those who *had* read the works in question often did not read them in their entirety before making sweeping statements like, "I can't use that in my congregation: the theology is so bad." In the case of *The Purpose Driven Life*, I have heard pastors note the exact day on which the "bad theology" appears (usually in the first week), complaining they cannot read past it.

Indeed, too often we read as critics rather than critically. We often never finish reading whole books and, as such, are unable to discuss them in depth or detail. It seems to matter little that *The Purpose Driven Life* has been one of the most widely read books and is repeatedly listed by Christians (regardless of theological persuasion) as one of, if not *the*, most influential book they have read.

I often wonder how much we so-called progressive, intellectual, theologically minded pastors trust our parishioners. Could it be that if we have been doing our jobs of helping people develop healthy, practical ("good?") theologies, we can entrust them to weed through that which may not be well-grounded?[4] Or perhaps we have been entrusting their theological development to whatever they can pick up and read on the market, and we do not trust them after all.

SEEKING APPROVAL

But this is about more than books. Often in transformational ministries, we hear comments like, "Has that program been approved by [insert your denomination's name here]?" or "Has that curriculum been written by [insert your denominational publishing house here]?" Interestingly, few people seem to be aware that some of our publishing houses no longer publish curricula, instead partnering with others. And many of our curricula options are no longer written in denominational vacuums: they are being written in collaboration with a number of folks from a widening variety of denominational representations. The questions no longer seem to fit today's denominational realities.

The fact remains, and with good reason, that people want to be assured that whatever we try will work, and somehow we connect blessed assurance to some amorphous, denominational stamp of approval. Let us say up front that these requests for assurance can be masqueraded attempts by some to redirect our attention and energy away from the transformational journey in any way they can. Otherwise, knowing what curriculum, program, or other ministry to buy or try is not an uncommon concern that can be a ticking time bomb, and it seems tempting to detonate this bomb when we find ourselves wandering around in the wilderness.

Bill Easum is a minister who spent twenty-four years leading the transformational journey of Colonial Hills United Methodist Church in San Antonio, Texas. His first book, *The Church Growth Handbook*,[5] was published in 1990. The next year the relatively innocuous *How to Reach Baby Boomers*[6] came out, but it was his controversial *Dancing with Dinosaurs: Ministry in a Hostile & Hurting World*[7] that gained him national notoriety. His next book, *Sacred Cows Make Gourmet Burgers*,[8] did little to further endear him to a reeling mainline audience.

Today Bill is one of the leading international consultants and advisors to mainline churches. We do not always like what he has to say or how he says it, but we do know that he speaks truthfully and from the Spirit; and we know that what he suggests works in the right places and under the right circumstances. Bill recognizes that he has always been a little edgy:

> During my early years of ministry at [Colonial Hills], my peers continually told me I was crazy because of the way I did ministry. My supervisors were always "on my case" because I was not following the denomination's way of doing things. Many of my peers referred to me as "the maverick," a term I came to cherish. In time, people began asking me what I was doing that caused the church in which I served Christ to grow.[9]

Indeed, congregational transformation is pretty "edgy." We always seem to be traveling at the edge of the wilderness and cannot generally predict what will meet us around the next corner. People who lead congregational transformation are a bit like cheerleading prophets, discerning the path and cheering us on, but often receiving little recognition for it.[10] When you are in a place of discernment and God's leading, you will find you may be ahead of, parallel to, or in seeming opposition to what your denomination is currently supporting.

And in response to those "looking for a sign," a stamp of approval, from their denomination, there is little to say. Denominations are huge machines that move slowly and shift even more laboriously; few are mobilized or staffed to help with congregational transformation. More than one judicatory is "figuring it out as we go along" and not many are staffed by people who have formal training in transformation beyond what they have read or discussed with peers. Perhaps their coveted stamp of approval is not really what we should be waiting for.

DISCERNMENT BEFORE DISMISSAL

So what are we to do about that dilemma of being open to resources that are produced beyond the walls of our denomination or theological persuasion? Indeed, there are a number of ideas and resources available to us. During our interviews with mainline pastors, Martha Grace Reese and I found that a number of them regularly attend conferences and workshops sponsored by nonmainline congregations. Many of us are aware of the vast array of Willow Creek[11] offerings: their popular workshops and seminars that draw people from around the world; their curricula and models for children, youth, and adult education; their communication tools; and their opportunities to network with others as part of the Willow Creek Association. Others of us have tapped into Saddleback and their offerings that branch beyond the popular Purpose Driven resources.

But many of us have gone outside the bounds of our denomination's offerings at the risk of great criticism and little support. Such border crossing seems to generate criticism and, I would suggest, springs from deep-seated fear. I am reminded of a congregation in a small, rural, midwestern town whose worship committee decided to try an Ash Wednesday service, a suggestion made by the new "citified" pastor (every church she had ever been a part of had observed it). None of the members in her current congregation had ever been to an Ash Wednesday service, and few knew anything about them beyond the realization that the Catholic Church up the street offered them every year.

Several of the members expressed a concern that the church might be incorporating Catholicism into their solid Protestant ways; a few other members made some of those proverbial pesky phone calls. While it had sounded like a good idea when the worship team presented it, a few calls from concerned members prompted the board chair to make his own phone call to the judicatory pastor "just to check" on whether or not observing Ash Wednesday was within the denomination's theology. The judicatory pastor wisely asked the board chair if he had access to a denominational calendar; yes, he did (the pastor had given one to each person on the board at the beginning of the year). The judicatory pastor then referred him to the February calendar and pointed out not only the marked date for Ash Wednesday but also the box with suggested resources for observing it. (Please notice: this is a positive example of judicatory support!)

So we do well to practice discernment before being dismissive. In the Pacific Northwest, for example, the evangelical church is growing by leaps and bounds while every mainline denomination declined between 1980 and 2000.[12] My own Disciples denomination accounted for 2.4 percent of Christians in the Pacific Northwest in 1980; in 2000 we accounted for only 0.7 percent.[13] However, we choose to talk *about* our evangelical sisters and brothers and to dismiss them and their constituencies and their methods carte blanche rather than talk *to* them and ask, "What are you doing that might also work for us?" or, "Is there anything we might be able to learn from you?" We have a hard time separating method from theology, but we are discovering that we are throwing babies out with what we have often prematurely judged to be dirty bathwater.

Taking What We Can Use

At the close of many Twelve Step meetings you will hear the statement, "Take what you need and leave the rest." Many congregations that are successfully reaching not-yet-Christians are ones that are open to drawing on nonmainline learnings and programs, which they adapt as necessary to their contexts. They take what they can use and leave the rest. This is particularly important because it has only been recently that any of our denominations have begun developing materials that speak to the needs of the not-yet-Christian population. A review of mainline curriculum in 2003 revealed less than a handful of adult resources that did not assume those adults had been raised in the church and had familiarity with core faith stories and spiritual disciplines such as prayer. Fortunately, we are seeing more resources for not-yet and new Christians, but this does not negate the potential relevance of nonmainline offerings. Alas, we often seem more ready to learn and link arms with those from non-Christian religions and in the secular world than we are to draw on our own tradition's resources or create new ones that reflect our beliefs.[14]

Paul's words to the congregation in Philippi are still valid for us today:

If then there is any encouragement in Christ, any consolation from love, any sharing in the Spirit, any compassion and sympathy, make my joy complete: be of the same mind, having the same love, being in full accord and of one spirit. Do nothing from selfish ambition or conceit, but in humility regard others as better than yourselves. Let each of you look not to your own interests, but to the interests of others.[15]

Paul's is a good reminder to let go of our vain conceit, our bent toward thinking we have a better, healthier version of the "Truth" that stands in opposition to "bad theology" and will somehow be tainted by it should "their" thinking come into contact with "ours."

A few years ago, a Disciples congregation that was working with a number of not-yet and new Christians decided to use Henry Blackaby's video study *Experiencing God.*[16] Judging by the weekly sessions, the group hated it and resorted to making fun of some of the phrases that popped up each week. After the pastor rethought his options and talked about them with the group, the group decided they wanted to persevere ("endure") through the entirety of the series. In retrospect, that pastor will tell you it was one of the best moves they made that year. It added breadth and depth to the participants' exposure to the Bible; they got a taste of a theology that was different from the one to which they were regularly exposed; and the pastor made sure they had opportunities to discuss, experiment with, and further explore their own theology in the mix of what they were learning. They were taking what they could use and in the process they gained clarity about what they themselves believed and why.

LOOKING FOR POTENTIAL

Not long ago, while visiting with recently ordained ministers, I suddenly realized we had slipped into a "bitch-fest," a round of increasing criticism and negative critique. A lot of us—particularly those of us who have gone to seminary—have been trained to be critical. However, we have a tendency to run with what we like—or don't like—and rapidly move into disapproval and even condemnation before taking time to step back and maintain some objectivity. We seem to be better trained at (and "rewarded" for) seeing problems than potential. We tend to be quick to judge and dismiss. But our survival depends in part on an ability to discern what is good and good for us to appropriate before dismissing as bad that which is foreign to us. There is, after all, more than one option when considering any kind of resource: excuse, edit, adapt, or adopt.

Discern before dismissing. Take what you need and leave the rest. Edit, adapt, adopt. By all means be critical in your discernment—but let's move beyond critique. We have too much work to do to waste time being critics.

In the end, all this is not about denominationalism: it is about the realm of God. For several years I have drawn upon the wealth and tradition of the Episcopalian *Book of Common Prayer* to guide and inform my morning and evening prayer times. The collect for Proper 16 speaks about unity:

> Grant, O merciful God, that your Church, being gathered together in unity by your Holy Spirit, may show forth your power among all peoples, to the glory of your Name; through Jesus Christ our Lord, who lives and reigns with you and the Holy Spirit, one God, for ever and ever. Amen.[17]

I wonder what might happen if *all* Jesus' Church became unified. I wonder what kind of power might shine forth through each of us and our churches, into our communities, and out into the world.

We have much to learn from our brothers and sisters of different Christian persuasions, and they, too, have some things they can learn from us. It is not that one is better or worse than the other, merely that we have different perspectives of the whole. In many respects, our thoughts about God are similar to the brilliance of a diamond. Like a diamond, comprising millions of facets, all the thoughts there have ever been about God and all the thoughts there will ever be about God will never capture the brilliance, the radiance, the whole of who God is. We each have a piece of the Truth—even those pieces that seem to be in conflict—and how much richer our thoughts about and our relationship with

God will be when we choose to wrestle and become open to stretching and being stretched.

When defusing time bombs in the transformational wilderness, we need all the resources and tools we can find, even those we might otherwise overlook. And how much surer our survival is when we move from being critics to critically starting to look for potential good.

Notes

1. Patricia O'Connell Killen and Mark Silk, *Religion and Public Life in the Pacific Northwest: The None Zone* (Creek, CA: AltaMira Press, 2004), 9.

2. Bruce Wilkinson, *The Prayer of Jabez: Breaking through to the Blessed Life* (Sisters, OR: Multnomah Publishers, 2000).

3. Rick Warren, *The Purpose Driven Life: What on Earth Am I Here For?* (Grand Rapids: Zondervan Publishing, 2002).

4. By no means am I suggesting that *The Purpose Drive Life,* or any other book, is not well-grounded.

5. Bill Easum, *The Church Growth Handbook* (Nashville: Abingdon Press, 1990).

6. Bill Easum, *How to Reach Baby Boomers* (Nashville: Abingdon Press, 1991).

7. Bill Easum, *Dancing with Dinosaurs: Ministry in a Hostile & Hurting World* (Nashville: Abingdon Press, 1993).

8. Bill Easum, *Sacred Cows Make Gourmet Burgers* (Nashville: Abingdon Press, 1995).

9. Bill Easum, *Leadership on the OtherSide: No Rules, Just Clues* (Nashville: Abingdon Press, 2000), 15.

10. See Mark 6:1–6.

11. Willow Creek Community Church is located in South Barrington, Illinois, outside of Chicago.

12. O'Connell Killen and Silk, *Religion and Public Life,* 33–35.

13. Ibid., 34.

14. I am thinking how many of us give hardly a second thought to drawing on the works of folks like the Dalai Lama or business gurus Jim Collins and Ronald Heifetz.

15. Philippians 2:1–4.

16. Henry Blackaby, *Experiencing God: Knowing and Doing the Will of God* (Nashville: Broadman & Holman Publishers, 1998).

17. *Book of Common Prayer*, "Proper 16," 232–33.

3

FIND THE RIGHT FITS

Improvise

Although my husband might disagree, I am not a shoe-horse. In reality, I am a pretty simple person and try to live a streamlined life, more out of necessity and convenience than natural inclination. As it is, it takes me enough time in the mornings to figure out what to wear, and I cannot imagine having to look through any more shoes than I have to decide which ones best coordinate with whatever I am wearing.

I do, though, have a small variety of shoes. There are three pairs of dress shoes: one in black, one in navy blue, and one in brown. I have two pairs of sandals for when it gets warm: a casual and a dress pair. I have a pair of tennis shoes for those days when I anticipate doing a lot of "running around." And, oh yes, I have three pairs of house shoes that people have given me. No matter how much I wish I could, I just cannot seem to get my shoe stable down to one or two pairs. Although I am most comfortable in my tennis shoes, I cannot imagine wearing them with my full Sunday preacher regalia, robe and stoles; likewise, I would not take a long, vigorous walk with heels on. In my line of work, shoes are not one-shoe-fits-all.

ONE SIZE DOES NOT FIT ALL

Similarly, the days of the "one-shoe-fits-all" for churches are over. The programs that fit the needs of one congregation may not meet the needs of the one across the street. A denominational stewardship program may work in some churches, but not necessarily in all (although many are now sensitive to demographic differences and are offering more varied options). Each congregation is unique: what is right for my setting is not necessarily right for yours.

A lot of us have discovered this one-size-does-not-fit-all principle the hard way by visiting a "successful" church and purchasing the rudiments of a program or two they were using and trying to implement it lock, stock, and barrel in our own congregations. Usually, the programs looked simple enough. After all, these congregations were using them successfully and everything purred along without a hitch. What we didn't realize was that the purr was actually a tick . . . as in a ticking time bomb.

For some of us, the explosions came sooner than later. We got frustrated in mid-excitement when we found that we did not have the talent pond (we only had a kiddy pool) to fully implement the ministry in our congregation. Others of us persevered for months, even years, before realizing that the exercises we had been working out of the workbooks were not getting us much farther than where we were when we started them. The questions were good and we usually had a good time with them, but they were not really taking us anywhere. In the end, a lot of us beat ourselves up: stupid choices, stupid people, stupid church, and stupid us for thinking our congregations could do or be better.

Take heart! Neither you nor your church is stupid. *Not every resource is appropriate for every congregation.*

Programs are like shoes: they are meant to take us places. Churches are living organisms that are meant to move. Sitting in one place too long leads to atrophy and life-threatening blood clots. We are meant to be in motion. That is why transformation is an ongoing journey, carrying us ever onward into eternity.

EVENTFUL LIVING

I have been working with a theory for some time that I call "eventful living." It suggests that many of us (at least in the United States and Canada) live life as a series of events with beginnings and ends. We start with early childhood whose end is marked by the beginning of preschool or kindergarten. Then come the "school years," which close with high school graduation. The next phase of life begins with starting a family and/or more school and/or delving into a job.

From here, the theory gets a bit more complicated: our lives and their paths and events are unique. But think about how we live our lives today. Forty years ago, people would likely retire from the job they had started forty years earlier; today it is predicted we will change not only jobs but *careers* numerous times before retirement. Today we find eventful living in many folks' work patterns. We work a job until it is time to have children and we need better income or benefits, or we switch to the career of child-raising. Others of us switch jobs when the children start school and/or leave the nest. Many of us take jobs to get what we want or to do what we have to (sometimes we are fortunate to get to do what we want). Pastors: a lot of us, too, have spent many years in eventful work: some of us are guilty of taking a church as a stepping stone to the "next one up."

Maybe all this is a coping mechanism. We figure we can do what we need to and put up with what we have to as long as we know (or hope) it will have an end. It helps us to face the long hours, days, and years of work that lie ahead. We are so geared into eventful living that weekends and holidays are capable of disrupting the patterns, and too many of us have no clue how to function when we do take a vacation. Perhaps the saddest part of eventful living, though, is that we lose sight of the bigger journey of life and all it holds for us. We get so focused on what we have to do to get through it that we are unable to see all that is trying to get through to us!

Churches also live eventfully, focusing on immediate events and losing sight and even memory of the greater journey. Weekly and monthly events like Sunday services and holidays and vacation Bible school take a lot of energy and attention. Yes, these are important events in our congregational lives, but be careful when they become coping mechanisms. Be careful when you find yourself thinking you can do what it takes to get through to the next Sunday, the next board meeting, the next holiday. As in our personal lives, eventful living helps our congregations face the long hours, drudging days, and (yawn!) years of work that lie ahead.

REALITY CHECK

If you find you are caught on the fast track to whatever is coming next (be it Sunday, a season, a vacation, or whatever), it's time for a reality check or two!

Reality Check 1: We are not meant to live from event to event: there is much more to life than that. Many of us are already experiencing the abundance and joy available to each one of us (and our congregations) when we are in an active relationship with God through Jesus Christ. That is what life is about: being in relationship with God, Jesus, and the Holy Spirit and with others . . . and living out what that means.

Reality Check 2: We do not have to live our lives as an endurance test; we really can move beyond the drudgery and exhausted enthusiasm to something better. BUT, we are going to have to step beyond eventful living and reengage the journey forward. If we do not, I guarantee you that next year will be no better than this.

So, how do we move on? How do we start journeying again? Or, for those of us who are already on the path, what do we need to do to journey a bit more efficiently? For starters, some of us are going to need some pretty heavy-duty hiking shoes at the start to get over the mountains and rocks surrounding us. Others of us are going to need steel-toed work boots to "kick some butt" and build some rock-solid foundations. Some of us may be ready for dancing shoes so that we can get on the relational dance floor and learn to adeptly waltz with all the different dance partners, especially the wallflowers, that a congregation provides. And some of us are going to need track shoes to get over the hurdles that keep getting in our way.

Transformation means we will have to identify and address the obstacles that have blocked our faithful journeys forward as congregations. There are a number of resources and programs available to assist us in that part of our transformational journeys, resources that will help us with obstacles such as faithful stewardship, conflict management, congregational grief and self-esteem, evangelism, mission and vision development, and more. Again, these are as varied as our respective congregations, so we need to consider, evaluate, and choose them carefully.

Transformation also rests on assuring, often developing, and continually assessing for good, solid, administrative and structural systems that allow ministry to stay relevant and vibrant; there are resources and programs available for that part of the journey. Transformation depends upon our ability to care for, talk to, disagree respectfully with, and grow with each person in the congregation; there are a number of other resources and programs available to assist us with that part of the journey.[1]

There are a lot of churches that are using programs to "bring in new people" through their front doors. But I get scared when I hear stories from pastors and other walking wounded about how people are treating one another behind the closed doors. I am sure you, too, have heard or told versions of character assassination, yelling-match board meetings, virulent phone calls, and poison-pen letters. Yet many of these churches are actively trying to get folks in the front door (usually to replace those that ran out the back door). For these congregations to put energy into evangelism is a dangerous waste of resources. If such congregations are serious about journeying forward, they first need resources that will allow them to create an environment of respect. We will say more about that in later chapters, but for now let us reiterate the importance of choosing the right shoe for the paths on which find ourselves.

TAKING THE CONFUSION OUT OF COORDINATING OUR SHOES

Alas, choosing and developing programs and ministries is one of the most confusing and misleading tasks we can encounter in transformation, and it is one of the most important tasks with which judicatory leaders can be charged. Here is a set of good basic questions to ask when considering a potential program or ministry:

1. What is holding us back from transforming? Are there issues or problems or situations we need to address?

2. With that in mind, what skills do we need to develop as a congregation? (Caution: it probably is not "how to invite people.")

3. How will this program or ministry help us do that as a congregation? How might it jeopardize us?

If your congregation owns (not merely has) its stated mission, vision, and values, then ask these additional questions:

4. How will this program or ministry further our mission and fulfill our vision? Does it reflect our values?

5. Can we afford it (in terms of human resources, creative resources, energy resources, geographical resources, and financial resources)?

Look at these questions realistically, without the Pollyanna rose-colored glasses. Refuse to get hooked by a bright and shiny program that you know won't fit your congregation. Be brutally realistic.

Many of us are grabbing programs and ministries off the shelves and World Wide Web in desperate attempts to "do something," anything, that will, at the very least, buy us time. But time is not cheap.

Remember, we are running out of money. What's more, our folks are running out of energy, enthusiasm, and excitement. The more we try and fail, the less enthusiastic and energized we are. And you can only muster so much excitement with each "new" idea, particularly when the previous ones burned dimly at best. And then there is the issue of trust. Sadly, this is one of the common concerns I hear in congregational consultations. People everywhere are concerned about whether or not their pastor "really does know what she [or he] is talking about." Congregational leaders do not know how much longer they can continue trying "one more thing," and they wonder if there is not some magical solution for them. Be realistic: is what you think is the next great program really going to be the solution to your congregation's ills, or is it only one more exercise in eventful living?

When I get up in the morning, I don't decide what shoes I want to wear and then choose my dress, slacks, or jacket. First, I decide what I will be doing that day and what I am going to wear: some days it's the heels, other days the tennis shoes, and some days we get to play and I try out golf or bowling shoes.

CHOICES

Recognizing the need for different programs and policies emerged early in the life of Christianity. The first Christians were Jews, so circumcision was of the utmost importance to them, a sign of their enduring covenant with God. Before long (as with any journey forward) a dilemma arose. As Christianity began to spread from the Jews to the Gentiles (anyone who was not a Jew), arguments broke out over the need for the new Gentile Christians to be circumcised. One of the apostles, Paul, had an uncircumcised Gentile traveling companion named Titus. Paul was another one of those "edgy" guys and a lot of folks held his ministry and methods as suspect to begin with. Partly because of Paul, and partly because of church tradition, the issue of circumcision became a huge issue for the growing church, particularly for its leadership in Jerusalem.

In the Newer Testament, we see Paul explain to the Gentile-Christians in Galatia: "We did not submit to them even for a moment, so that the truth of the gospel might always remain with you."[2] And we know that after conferring with the pillars of the church (James, Peter, and John), Paul and his companions were given the green light to continue their ministry without the need to impose circumcision on anyone. Indeed, we learn from Paul: "They asked only one thing, that we remember the poor."[3]

It is not as though Paul was against circumcision; after all, he himself was circumcised. In fact, we know he found it important enough to circumcise another Gentile disciple, Timothy, when the nature of the ministry they were pursuing necessitated it.[4] Circumcision moved from a rite, an event, to a tool: a shoe for walking down certain paths. When the shoe of circumcision fit—as it did for Timothy—they used it. When it didn't—as with Titus—they did not.

My husband and I pastored two different churches that were four blocks apart on Main Street in a small, rural, Kansas town. What worked in the Disciples congregation I pastored was not feasible for the Presbyterian congregation my husband pastored—not because they were in different denominations but because the dispositions and callings of the congregations were different. There were, of course, some ministries they could and did share with other denominations: a community-wide Vacation Bible school on the county courthouse lawn in the center of town, the Holy Week lunches, and other joint worship opportunities.

But the Bible study at my pastorate was necessarily different than the studies my husband was engaging in his pastorate up the street, not for the sake of preference but because the two had different foci and needs. In fact, the other Presbyterian church my husband was also pastoring, this one seventeen miles away, regularly engaged in yet different studies and used different programs and ministry techniques to reach the people in their community. Considering those two yoked Presbyterian congregations, one might think on the surface that they could use similar programs or approaches; after all, they were both located in small, declining, rural towns built around ranching and farming. But they could not: not effectively.

Choosing programs and developing ministries cannot be done outside the context of our congregation's transformational journey. It takes particular equipment and preparation to problem solve, and this problem solving "must be based on recognizing threats to your life, knowing their priority of influence, knowing their severity of threat to your life, and taking actions that will keep you alive."[5] When called to defuse a bomb, the bomb squad must first analyze with what kind of device they are contending before choosing a course of action. Defusing a chemical explosive calls for different techniques than defusing a thermobaric or hydrogen bomb.

Sometimes the bomb squad has to call in an expert or two. Our congregations can benefit from trained judicatory staff members who have the call, capability, ability, capacity, and passion to work with congregations on an individual level, helping them to discover and unleash their potentials. This is a shift from judicatory ministers trying to make an appearance in each congregation sometime every year or two (or three or five) to spending significant time with each congregation's leadership to help them assess their journey and needs.

Another one of my favorite "events" in the Bible is found in the sixteenth chapter of the book of Acts.[6] Here, Paul and his companions had been traveling throughout Phrygia and Galatia (now Turkey), hoping to journey to Asia. Try as they might, though, they just couldn't make their way over the border into Asia; each of their attempts to cross into the province was somehow thwarted. One night, Paul had a dream in which a Macedonian begged Paul to come to Macedonia. The next day, Paul and his companions were able to journey forward once again, only this time in a slightly different direction.

I cannot begin to tell you how many times I have found myself sitting at a transformational border, or crossroad, seemingly unable to move forward. With that has often come the prayer, "Oh, God: could you hurry up and get us there!?!" Sometimes that prayer comes with negative thoughts, imaginations, and fears: maybe this congregation was not meant to transform, maybe I am not up to the task, maybe "they" are not up to the task. Walking amidst the potential programmatic time bombs of the transformational journey challenges us to be patient, creative, and improvisational; but, more importantly, it calls us to the crucial task of recognizing the threats to our lives, prioritizing their influence and severity of threat, and choosing which actions to take to address and overcome them. We have to find the right program that will fit our particular needs. Then we will be able to choose what shoes we need to wear.

Notes

1. Transformation, of course, depends on much more than these three parts; but I don't want to get sidetracked by discussing other aspects here.

2. Galatians 2:5.

3. Galatians 2:10.

4. Acts 16:1–5.

5. *Wilderness Survival*, "Preparing Yourself," http://www.wilderness-survival .net/mind-3.php.

6. Acts 16:6–10.

4

PUT THE RIGHT PEOPLE IN THE RIGHT PLACES

While still living in Seattle, my husband, Bill, and I attended a conference in downtown Charlotte, North Carolina. Someone else had made and paid for our motel arrangements, which were several miles out of the city center but on a convenient bus route. Bill was working on a project and needed several items we were unable to pack into our suitcases, so one of our first tasks was to find a store there. We were able to locate one, but it was not conveniently situated on the bus line. We asked how far a walk it was and were told it was a little over a mile and one-half away: no problem for walkers like us! So we set out. Two hours later we arrived at our destination. It may have been a two-mile drive at one time, but it was more like a six-mile hike once we navigated and circumvented the new highway that was being built. To add insult to injury, it was in the nineties (hotter than heck for Seattleites) and my feet were more in need of hiking boots than neighborhood walking shoes.

That two-hour foray plagued me for several months to come. Most immediately, I had blisters in several spots on both feet that got raw and ached the whole time we were in Charlotte, and I hobbled around the conference. The blisters got infected and festered, and I finally figured out that I had worn a corn on one of my toes—something I never had experienced before and would have to endure for what seemed like forever.

For months it did not matter what shoes I wore; every pair seemed to exacerbate the problems.

Now, you may be thinking, "TMI" ("too much information")! You do not need the graphic, oozing details of my feet. But my point is that it really does not matter what shoes we wear in our congregations—what programs we use—when we have open, festering sores on our feet.

OPEN SORES

What kind of sores does your congregation have? One of the biggest rubs, inflictors of sores, in the transformational congregation is mean people. Most of you know what I am talking about . . . many of you are already identifying specifically about *whom* I am talking.

Perhaps you have your own variation of Willy Jones (not his real name, at least not to me). He is one of the crankiest, most cynical persons to cross the threshold of the church. But cross he does, nearly every day. He is there whenever you need something, and even when you don't. He does not tend to say much—it is more like a grumble—but when he does, watch out because it is more than likely you have forgotten to turn off a light, have used too much toilet paper, or have moved a serving cart in the kitchen.

It does not seem to matter that people complain about his meanness, or that he has been responsible for chasing off no fewer than five prospective members with his barking reminders, or that he repeatedly breaks confidentiality by sharing whom he sees behind the pastor's office doors. I say, "It does not seem to matter" because the congregation's leadership has a way of making excuses when the pastor requests that they address the issue (since his addressing it with Willy has so far gone unheeded). Or maybe they do not directly excuse Willy's behavior, instead redirecting the pastor's concerns with questions like "Who else will do what he does for us?" Rather than addressing the issue and risk making the Willies and Wilmas in our congregations mad and running them off, we allow these folks to continue doing their damage.

KINDNESS DOES NOT EQUAL NICENESS

We need a lot of folks to do a lot of work around the church, but not "just anybody" can—or should—do anything, let alone everything. And *never* should festering folk be allowed to ooze on, or infect, other people or ministries.

I know this is not easy. I hate confrontation. My natural inclination is to avoid it, but I have learned it is generally easier to take care of it up front. On one hand, I do not spend inordinate amounts of time playing out (and dreading) possible scenarios in my head. On the other hand, when we address what needs to be addressed when it needs to be addressed, we go a long way to preventing infection and potential loss of limbs.

A friend in Missouri regularly says that we in the church fail to confront meanness. Another friend aptly reminds folks that there is a difference between "being kind" and "being nice." Bill Easum adds:

> I'm convinced that most church people think that one of the tenets of Christianity is being nice. Too many church people think pastors should be nice people and churches are supposed to be nice places where people live harmoniously together. As a result, most church leaders never really say what they feel or think, which leads to a loss of community and a handful of dysfunctional controllers who keep the majority of people intimidated. Niceness leads to the withholding of information, manipulation of people and events, and gossip. I've discovered that the most dangerous gatekeepers often appear to be nice.[1]

One of the first disagreements I had with my father was during a fourth-grade Sunday school class in which he was the teacher and I was a student. That particular Sunday we were reading the account of Jesus clearing out the money changers and merchants in the temple area.[2] As was our class custom, we were reading out of our Sunday school pamphlets rather than the Bible, so all we had for reference was the pamphlet and my father's teaching. I was appalled by the lesson that day and challenged my dad there in front of my classmates: "That's not true," I blurted out.

"What do you mean?" my father asked.

"Jesus would never get mad; he couldn't be so mean. There is no way he would do something like that."

Thirty-three years later, I was grateful for my friend's understanding that kindness does not equal niceness.

FACING FESTERING FOLK

As I mentioned earlier, Bill Easum's methods and modes of delivery are not always greatly appreciated; but few can dispute that he is a wise man. Whenever he is asked how to handle festering folk, he responds: "Convert them, neutralize them, or kick them out."[3] To the typical response, "That's not Christian!" Bill typically responds, "What they mean is, 'That's not very nice.'"[4]

Indeed, the *kindest* thing we can do for people is to call them on their meanness. Some of them are unaware of how their words, actions, and reactions are being received by others. I have coached a number of pastors and leaders who have ADHD[5] (both diagnosed and undiagnosed). One of the consequences for ADHD adults is that they have not adequately learned how to read social cues. As such, they do not always have the keenest sense of when they are offending someone.[6]

In all but one case, those with whom I have had to have conversations about negative or unhelpful behaviors have welcomed the observation that their manners were less than loving. Was it easy to tell them? No. I agonized over it for days, praying to find the *nicest* way to say what needed to be said.

Was I mean when I spoke with them? Few people consider me a "mean" person but, rather, one who wants nothing but the best for people and churches; that helps with credibility. Also, I approach these tough conversations from a place of humility and curiosity (as opposed to inquisition): "Have you noticed a disconnection between you and so-and-so?" "Have you taken any time to think about the reactions you have been getting when you say thus-and-such?" Questions like these have opened the door for what are now established, enduring relationships of trust and authentic discipleship.

FAITHFULLY SERVING THOSE WE SERVE

Indeed, pastors and leaders are entrusted with the responsibility of helping people with their spiritual journeys, and that means helping them grow into faithful discipleship.[7] To be specific, discipling entails:

1. Helping people to live into a transformational relationship with God and others through Jesus Christ

2. Helping them discover their spiritual gifts and passions

3. Helping them realize how God might be calling them to use those gifts to help reveal a piece of the reign of heaven here on earth, particularly to those who have not yet glimpsed it

4. Equipping them to continually develop and use those gifts both inside and beyond the church doors

5. Releasing them to serve God and be the tangible touch of Jesus for others: revealing God's realm, inviting others to be a part of it, and engaging the work of discipling.

Bruce Humphrey, the senior pastor at Rancho Bernardo Community Presbyterian Church (USA), offers that pastors and leaders are here to serve folks by helping them serve God's realm; the folks in the pews are not here to serve us, the leadership.⁸ If we are going to serve them by helping them to be the best servants they can be, we are going to have to help them refine their rough spots (just as we have to work on our own). Whenever we allow people to act out, to control, to be mean, infectious, or oozing with anything contrary to love, we are not growing disciples: we are breeding monsters.

Throughout the Bible we find lists of appropriate and inappropriate behaviors for followers of Jesus Christ. I like to use them as barometers of where we are in our spiritual journeys. When people ask me, "How can I tell if I am growing in my faith?" I often refer them to the fifth chapter of Galatians. Many of us can recite the fruits of the spirit that are listed there in verses 22 and 23 (love, joy, peace, patience, kindness, goodness, faithfulness, gentleness, and self-control in the NIV).⁹ However, few of us are familiar with the "obvious" rotting, fleshy stuff in verses 19–21: sexual immorality, impurity, and debauchery; idolatry and witchcraft; hatred, discord, jealousy, fits of rage, selfish ambition, dissensions, factions, and envy; drunkenness, orgies, and the like.

One of the boldest moves I have witnessed in a congregation was taken by two of the nicest, most loving congregational leaders you could ever hope to meet, a man and a woman who were, respectively, the chair of the church elders and the chair of the board. In that church there were two deacons who, along with their wives, had been sowing seeds of hatred, discord, dissension, and factioning since the pastor's arrival fifteen months earlier. This was in a family-sized congregation located in a declining small town where people fought like cats and dogs but made up as quickly as children because their existence depended on one another. Meanness and overlooking it were a way of life for many of the town folks.

At the start of one year's nominating process, the pastor challenged the nominating committee to measure all prospective nominees by the fruits of the spirit evident in them. When the committee got to filling the deacon "slots," the names of the two deacons were automatically put back on the roster because of their years of service and the fact that "there would be hell to pay" if they were missing from the proposed slate. "What 'fruit' do you see in them?" the pastor asked. They all admitted they did not see any fruit, although the committee acknowledged that in earlier days the two had "had their moments" and still had fruity potential.

The matter was referred to the pastoral advisory committee, who agreed that the men were displaying rotting flesh rather than fruit. The committee determined they could not in good conscience recommend that the men return as deacons. This was, of course, quite a dilemma. There sure would be hell to pay: it would be disruptive to the forward movements the congregation had been making, and the men and their families would probably leave the church. Yet, the pastoral advisory committee could not reconcile any of that with the message they would be sending to the congregation if they endorsed unhealthy people serving in leadership positions. Beyond that, they realized they were doing the men no favors by allowing their mean behavior to continue without addressing it; that would not be kind.

Subsequently, the board and elder chairs made appointments to visit with each of the deacons. In both cases, they spoke of the men's gifts and what the elders perceived as their potentials for leadership (the one deacon clearly had suppressed gifts for being an elder). They also explained to the men why their names would not be appearing on the roster of nominees that year, and suggested ways they could work on the behaviors and grow in their love for God and others. The meetings were held conversationally, in as kind and loving ways as possible; and they were not easy. It took a few debriefing sessions for the chairs to feel comfortable with what they had done, although they knew all along it was what they needed to do. Coming out of that experience, they were stronger and bolder in their ability to be kind and to truly lead the church and disciple its participants. In fact, today they remain two of the most respected and admired people in town.

As suspected, the two families left, but they went to a church down the road that was known for building disciples. The seeds had been planted and they found themselves in a congregation that loved them, yet was cautious about moving them into leadership, and nurtured them into their potential and possibilities.

Adults can be like children who throw temper tantrums: they continue to kick and scream until we either address the matter at hand or they fall asleep. The differences are that adults are bigger; have longer memories and, as such, more endurance; and have garnered years of meaner, more inappropriate behaviors to fuel their tantrums. To ignore them is to exacerbate the problem for ourselves and for our congregations . . . and we do a great disservice to those who are throwing the tantrums. In reality, our attempts to ignore the tantrums boil down to our ignoring the sources of people's pain or, probably more accurately, their inability to appropriately express their anger, frustration, or whatever it may be.

If we are going to take seriously our responsibility to disciple people (which is an inherent part of the transformational journey), we are going to have to get past their kicking and screaming and move into a relationship with them that will allow us to address rotting fleshy stuff and their lack of awareness, lack of training, lack of willingness—whatever it is that prevents them from growing in love. We will also need to be ready to make suggestions and/or referrals so their own transformations won't remain at a screeching halt. Perhaps it will be time for them to take a detour. Whether or not they choose to give up their bombs, we have the responsibility to remove and defuse them before they can do more harm.

FROM GOOD TO GREAT

But we digress. This chapter is not about the wrong people in the right places, it is about putting the right people into the right places. Chapter 3 of the classic *Good to Great* by Jim Collins (about companies that have transitioned and sustained their excellence) is dedicated to this topic. In it, he uses the metaphor of a bus ride for describing this aspect of the transformational journey and notes that the executives who ignited the transformations from good to great did not first figure out where to drive the bus and then get people to take it there. No, they *first* got the right people on the bus (and the wrong people off the bus) and *then* figured out where to drive it. In essence they said, "Look, I don't really know where we should take this bus. But I know this much: If we get the right people on the bus, the right people in the right seats, and the wrong people off the bus, then we'll figure out how to take it someplace great."[10]

Putting the right people in the right places is more important than choosing the right program because programs matter little if we do not have the right people (not person) to administer and minister to them (and we are not just talking about the talent pool).

You may be thinking that Jim Collins' corporate observations have little to do with congregations, so let us consider for a moment a study by Thom Rainer. Thom looked at more than fifty thousand churches to find those that met his criteria for a "breakout church," meaning churches that (1) were consistently evangelistic as evidenced by at least twenty-six conversions a year since their "breakout year"; (2) averaged at least a one-year conversion ratio of no more than 20:1 (twenty members to one new convert) since its breakout year; (3) were declining or plateaued for several years before their breakout; (4) broke their "slump" and had been sustaining growth for several years; (5) had retained the same pastor from before and through the breakout (that is, without a change in leadership); and (6) were having a "clear and positive impact on the community" since the breakout point.[11]

In each of these "break-out" churches, Thom Rainer and his team discovered principles for breaking out that parallel the findings by Jim Collins and his team, among them, that the pastors in these breakout churches surrounded themselves with the "right" people, although they may not have known at the time what the "right" places were going to look like for those people. Thom notes that

> breakout church leaders often do not wait for an opening be-
> fore bringing a person on staff or providing a place for a lay
> leader to serve. If they come across a promising individual, they
> invite him or her to join the team even if there is no clear place
> for the person at that time. It typically does not take long before
> that capable and motivated person is making a difference in the
> church using his or her God-given gifts and abilities.[12]

The ways in which room has been made for me in ministry tells me this observation is true.

My first pastor, Charles S. Crenshaw, followed up with this twenty-two-year-old not-yet-professed Christian who responded to his sermon one Sunday morning and expressed an interest in "doing something with the youth in the neighborhood"; it was the first time I had been anywhere near a church in more than three years. Although I had only a GED, had lived on the streets for two years, and had little work experience past bad waitressing, fast food, and working as a maid, Charles saw something in me that I would not see in myself for a long time.

Rather than put me to work immediately with the youth or children, Charles asked if I would be interested in cleaning the library that had not been used in years. I cleaned and organized the library and moved on to the other rooms in the unused portions of the building, spending hours at the near-dead inner-city church. A couple of weeks later, Charles asked if I knew how to type and file; I knew how to type and figured I could figure out filing: "It's A-B-C, isn't it?" It was; and I did; and soon I was learning how to type bulletins, run a mimeograph machine, and fold and mail newsletters. Within two months I was the church's part-time secretary, which led to an opportunity to revive (and later become the director of) the church's food pantry program.

At the same time, Charles had not forgotten my desire to work with the youth in our neighborhood. Almost immediately he was sending me—usually "taking me" because I did not drive—to every training event our denomination offered: youth ministry, children's ministry, evangelism, stewardship, and more. That fall, with a couple of workshops under my belt, I apprenticed with a seasoned Sunday school saint who taught the three children in fourth through sixth grades (and me, who needed to learn most of the Bible stories). I also took my first steps into leading youth ministry. The next summer I codirected vacation Bible school. I was given the opportunity to serve in worship and to sometimes lead Bible study for the women's group. All along, Charles provided me with resources, reflected with me, and taught me from his own wisdom and experience.

That kind of mentoring/apprenticing relationship continued with two[13] of the three pastors who followed Charles Crenshaw: Douglas Brown and Ewell Hardman.[14] Yet another pastor who became a member at that church, Hal Knight, also mentored and encouraged me. At least six times every year, I was at everything from half-day to day-long to weekend-long training opportunities. The sharing, support, and opportunities these pastors provided me opened doors beyond belief: they walked me to and through college. After seven years with that congregation I went on to create and develop the lead staff position in children's and youth ministries for a large suburban congregation.

Many of us in congregational leadership find ourselves in two desperate situations: we have key slots to fill and we need leaders to lead the programs we think will transform our congregations. But remember to hone in on the *right* people first, even if they may not fit your perceived plan. And what you need for now, the holding environment you are wanting to create, is one with a few, well-grounded, growing disciplers. They may not have it all together, but they will be willing to work toward it.

FINDING THE RIGHT PEOPLE

Jim Collins notes that a key part of going from good to great (we will say, to *transforming*) is "creating a culture of discipline":

> It all starts with disciplined *people*. The transition begins not by trying to discipline the wrong people into the right behaviors, but by getting *self-disciplined* people on the bus in the first place. Next we have disciplined *thought*. You need the disci-

pline to confront the brutal facts of reality, while retaining reso-
lute faith that you can and will create a path to greatness. Most
importantly, you need the discipline to persist in the search for
understanding.[15]

Go slowly (and, yes, you have time, no matter how quickly it *seems*
to be running out). Look for disciplined people who have the *potential*
to disciple others. It helps to build relationships with students at Bible
colleges and seminaries (many of whom need "internship" opportunities) and with pastors, particularly of large churches, who often have a
large pond and may be willing to "lend you" some folks. Be creative but
avoid promising money, something that always seems to be in short sup-
ply. Do not forget, though, to be open to suggestions for creative funding; just be sure to let the suggestion-maker do the research, and *keep
your leadership team in the loop*: this is about the *congregation*, not
about you! Finally, remember to develop your own leadership team.
Pastors, invite your leaders into times for worship and study and prayer
with you. Leaders, invite your pastors to join *you*! Become grounded
together!

So now we have considered wrong people in the right places and at-
tracting the right people for the right places, but what about all the other
folks we already have? The truth is, we often approach "doing church"
from the perspective that we do not have the same selective luxury as
corporations when it comes to driving the bus. In other words, we are
"stuck" with the folks we have. In some ways, that is true; but it is unfair
and unrealistic to think of ourselves as "stuck."

The reality is that each one of us *has* been given gifts by God to serve
as the body of Christ, offering the tangible touch of Jesus to all we meet
and greet. Maybe you have heard this popular passage from the first letter the apostle Paul wrote to the people in Corinth:

Indeed, the body does not consist of one member but of many.
If the foot would say, 'Because I am not a hand, I do not belong
to the body,' that would not make it any less a part of the body.
And if the ear would say, 'Because I am not an eye, I do not belong to the body,' that would not make it any less a part of the

body. If the whole body were an eye, where would the hearing be? If the whole body were hearing, where would the sense of smell be? But as it is, God arranged the members in the body, each one of them, as he chose.[16]

It tends to be a favorite. However, we often forget some of the latter parts of the chapter, where we read:

On the contrary, the members of the body that seem to be weaker are indispensable, and those members of the body that we think less honorable we clothe with greater honor, and our less respectable members are treated with greater respect; whereas our more respectable members do not need this. But God has so arranged the body, giving the greater honor to the inferior member, that there may be no dissension within the body, but the members may have the same care for one another. If one member suffers, all suffer together with it; if one member is honored, all rejoice together with it.

Now you are the body of Christ and individually members of it. And God has appointed in the church first apostles, second prophets, third teachers; then deeds of power, then gifts of healing, forms of assistance, forms of leadership, various kinds of tongues.[17]

For a number of years I have been helping people explore, discover, and figure out how to best use their spiritual gifts and passions. It took a while, though, to get a unique perspective on individual gifts and passions and their role in a congregation. One afternoon I sat with a pastor and the Personal Ministry Assessments[18] for his team of elders. What emerged was a kaleidoscope of ministry possibilities waiting to happen if the elders would only step up to the plate and share their gifts of teaching, healing, helping, and administration. And that did not take into account the gifts of those in the congregation at large!

Beyond ignorance, there appear to be four reasons we do not pursue discovering the gifts and passions of our folks: (1) time, (2) making it a priority, (3) a realized inability to do anything with our discoveries, and

(4) fear of what we might find. Indeed, I am often asked the question about what you do with people "who have no gifts" or who have "no ministry potential."

First, let me say that *everyone* has gifts, usually more than one! I have seen people whom churches have relegated to the pews for years because of "their mental states" or "age" or "fill-in-your-own-apprehension" become well-functioning limbs of the body. Some have had the gift of assistance and have overcome fear and apprehension to answer phones for a couple of hours a week; some make phone calls to shut-ins; others send birthday cards on behalf of the church[19]; others are cooks with gifts of hospitality and bring great joy by fixing folks' favorite dishes; some write poetry to share in the newsletter, Bible studies, and even in worship services; some stand or sit near the doors greeting people. You get the picture.

Somewhere along the line, we in the church have hierarchically prioritized roles and positions and assigned to certain ones of them honor rather than recognizing them all for what they are: equal opportunities to give of ourselves. Too many of us have spent far too much time begging, cajoling, and even bargaining with people to fill slots rather than lovingly encouraging, nurturing, and supporting them—building their confidence and ability—to use their gifts and unleash their ministry passion and potential. Our congregations would be happier and healthier if people were enabled to work within their gift-mixes and passions rather than to work out their frustrations.

The need to figure out the right place for each person is crucial for holding our transformational journeys. On the one hand, it releases our congregation's ministry potential. On the other hand, it helps to avoid potential ministry disasters. Some of you have heard the story about the relatively new Christian who was a young, talented computer whiz—an introvert by the way—who told his pastor he had some spare time he would like to give to the church. Knowing the youth group was without a sponsor, the pastor immediately blurted out that the fellow would be the perfect youth sponsor because, of course, he was young and wanted to "do something." The young man, wanting very much to be involved (and trusting the pastor), said, "Sure!" Six months later the man was nowhere to be found. If the pastor had taken the time to look, he would have found the young man burned out and feeling like a failure. The youth were again without a leader and feeling disenfranchised.

This is yet one more example of putting the right person in the wrong place. The young man had a lot to offer *in another setting* (perhaps in helping upgrade the church's computer or updating the database or website), one that would have fit his personality type, gifts, and passion.

We need the right people in the right places. And to those of you who think or fear you cannot do something, whether it is the tough work of confrontation or confronting our perceived inadequacies or defusing a time bomb, I respond that the goal is not to eliminate our fears but to build confidence in our ability to function despite them. Explode your doubts and expand your future! Let God use you.

Notes

1. Easum, *Leadership on the OtherSide: No Rules, Just Clues* (Nashville: Abingdon Press, 2000), 160.

2. See Mark 11:15–17; Matthew 21:12–13; Luke 19:45–46; and John 2:13–16.

3. I have heard Bill say this many times over the years, but you can read it for yourself in *Leadership on the OtherSide,* 161.

4. Ibid.

5. Attention deficit hyperactivity disorder.

6. Of course, there are others who do not have ADHD or anything like it who unwittingly offend: some are extreme introverts, others are moving at such lightning speed they do not take the time to register what happens in their wake, and still others have not been attuned to healthy social interactions.

7. Those of us in the Christian Church (Disciples of Christ) will note this is "little 'd'" disciples, not "Big 'D'" Disciples.

8. Bruce made this observation several times while I was spending time with him and his staff on 5 October 2004 and during the weekend of 8–10 October 2004.

9. The New Revised Standard Version of the Bible exchanges "generosity" for "goodness."

10. Jim Collins, *Good to Great: Why Some Companies Make the Leap . . . and Others Don't* (New York: HarperBusiness, 2001), 41.

11. Thom S. Rainer, *Breakout Churches: Discover How to Make the Leap* (Grand Rapids: Zondervan, 2005), 20–21.

12. Ibid., 92.

13. The other pastor was a short-term interim when my second child was born, so we did not have much opportunity to connect.

14. While reticent to name too many names herein, particularly because I do not want to dishonor anyone by not mentioning them by name, these three men were pivotal in my early professional and expanding personal journey and have served as key models for how I minister and coach ministry. I owe them a debt of gratitude and thanksgiving.

15. Collins, 126.

16. 1 Corinthians 12:14–20.

17. 1 Corinthians 12:22–28.

18. The Personal Ministry Assessment is a tool I developed with input from my husband that helps people think about what God may be preparing them for, or calling them to do, within the context of their spiritual gifts, personality preferences, passions, and experiences.

19. In one church, the elders provided a woman in her nineties with the birthday list, cards, and address labels each month so that her writing was minimized. This became a wonderful ministry for her and provided the elders an opportunity to visit monthly with a very proud woman living at home on her own who refused to be considered as a "shut-in."

5

Keep Cool, Calm, and Collected

have been known to describe myself as a Type A+++, overachieving, perfectionist. I graduated from college as the mother of three children under the age of ten, in the top tenth of my class, with high honors, and was inducted into Mortar Board and Phi Beta Kappa. I was invited into the honors program in seminary, took PhD-level Newer Testament courses as a masters student, and graduated magna cum laude while blending a new family with five children, carrying eighteen to twenty-two academic hours a semester during my final two years of seminary, enduring a ten-month unpaid student-chaplaincy at a VA hospital, interning another semester at my home church, cofounding and directing a community-wide helping agency in the town where my husband was pastoring, and all along working at least one job to help make ends meet. I graduated from the doctor of ministry program as a Bakke Scholar with a 4.0 GPA.

Process

I must confess that it has only been in the past four years that have I begun to pace myself and appreciate days off (neither an easy task); and I am currently trying to figure out what "vacationing" looks like for me. I am not one to sit idly by. But I do not share all this to impress you, generate sympathy, or otherwise give you insight into the darker parts of my psyche. Rather, I share it to say that I know what it is like to run hard and fast. I am an idea person, and much of my life has been marked by having a goal in mind and determinedly striving for it. I am known for an ability to analyze and solve problems and to successfully complete that which I set out to do.

But, somewhere along the line I have had to learn about *process.* Becoming a process person has not come naturally for me; I function more readily in solution mode. My first real introduction to it came during an upper-level sociology class in college. We had a new instructor who approached teaching from the perspective of preparing us for graduate school. As such, we were expected to read the day's readings and come to class with questions and comments on what we'd read; learning, then, was intended to emerge out of our class discussions.

The instructor's method confounded and frustrated me: I wanted "the answers," and I expected her to tell me what I needed to know and do. I have no aversion to reading and thinking, but I wanted the professor to build on it and to assure me that I wasn't thinking too far afield. And anyway, what did I, or any of my classmates, in our ignorance have to add to the experience? I wanted the instructor to come in with the outline, fill my head with knowledge and practical examples, respond to questions, and give me an opportunity to synthesize and further explore in papers and on tests.

I think I had a better appreciation for process by the time I graduated, but I did not become aware of my relying on it until a few years back when I caught myself promoting the power of process to frustrated folks who were bent on results *now*. In truth, I think I made the leap to having to rely on process during a looooong twenty-six months in a desolate pastoral wilderness. I learned a number of helpful things during that pastorate: things like conflict management, the fact that search committees do not always represent the views or desires of the rest of the congregation, and my need to be within eight hours of large bodies of water with tides.

With the help of a spiritual director, I learned something about patience by learning to live and find things to celebrate in the now, rather than focusing my every conscious moment on hopes and dreams that are in some as-yet-unfulfilled future. I also learned the significance of spending time each day in prayer and Bible study, and to this day I follow a discipline of morning and evening prayer to keep me grounded and mindful of God's greater journey. And in that desert time, I came to value and look forward to three or more hours a week in contemplative, silent, still prayer where I have at times profoundly found myself in God's presence.

We have already said that much of what we are talking about in this book is the creation of environments for holding transformation. We could call such environments holding spaces, or, metaphorically, oases: fertile havens, environments, of sanctuary and safety. For those of us engaging the transformational journey in congregations, these holding spaces are more than merely places for holding transformation; they are places where we can safely cool down, freshen up, rest, and refuel.

You may be familiar with the stress indicator tests that assign numerical values to a variety of positive and negative stressors we are likely to encounter in our lives. These indicators have been designed to help us monitor the amount of stress we encounter and to become savvy about taking on too much stress, which contributes to emotional, mental, relational, spiritual, and/or professional breakdowns. I giggle when I think of a few items we might add to the Congregational Stress Indicator:

- Add 50 points if you are in a transformational congregation.

- Add 100 points if you are leading a congregational transformation.

- Add 500 points if your best friend recently left your congregation.

- Add 1,000 points if you are wandering in a transformational wilderness.

Heifetz and Linsky talk about the importance of pacing work, reminding us that people can handle only so much change at one time. Yet pacing work is often difficult both because of our commitment and because the enthusiasm of those with whom we work can push us ahead. Consequently, Heifetz and Linsky also remind us that pacing work is an improvisational art: "Not only must you be open to the possibility of changing course in midstream, you should expect that after seeing people's reactions, you will have to reassess and take ongoing corrective action."[1]

If you have not done so already, I encourage you to read their *Leadership on the Line* for yourself, but first I want to make the point that it is crucial to know how much to push, how to push, and when to push. And all that demands making time along the way to monitor, monitor, monitor, and to plan for oases and opportunities to cool down and regain composure.

Yet by taking breaks, we risk losing momentum and sight of the prize. Our oases become diversions rather than disciplined, intentional times of rest and respite. As a result, we can find ourselves months into an oasis with our transformational process detoured or, worse yet, derailed.

In the last chapter, I talked about the importance of a culture of discipline. A vital aspect of that discipline is *focus*. In chapter 6 of *Good to Great,* Jim Collins shares an overview of Lee Iacocca's rise and fall at Chrysler (or, perhaps more accurately, Chrysler's rise and fall with Lee Iacocca). In the first half of Iacocca's time at Chrysler's helm, his discipline and focus took the company from near-bankruptcy to the top of the industry. However, about halfway in,

> Iacocca seemed to lose focus and the company began to decline once again. The *Wall Street Journal* wrote: "Mr. Iacocca headed the Statue of Liberty renovation, joined a congressional commission on budget reduction and wrote a second book. He began a syndicated newspaper column, bought an Italian villa where he started bottling his own wine and olive oil. . . . Critics contend it all distracted him, and was a root cause of Chrysler's current problems. . . . Distracting or not, it's clear that being a folk hero is a demanding sideline."[2]

Discipline and focus are paramount for sustained, and sustaining, transformation. Oases breaks—rest and Sabbath-keeping—are part of the discipline of keeping focused, but some of us get distracted and we veer from Sabbath to sidelined. There is a fine line between the discipline of Sabbath that allows us to remain focused and the diversions and redirections of our ministries that, if we are not careful, cause us to lose sight of the transformational journey. Remember, the oases are an integral part of the journey, places of holding—not detours!

TRAVELING UNCHARTED TERRITORY

In many respects, the transformational journey is like traveling uncharted territory: we have some insights and reports and suggestions for maneuvering along the terrain, but it is a unique adventure for each of us. Never mind that we have a perceived destination in mind: the journey is full of peaks and pits, natural and unnatural disasters, and a host of divergent paths and detours.

But we are not without resources. In fact, we find in chapter 27 of the Newer Testament book of Acts a number of ways we can approach such uncharted circumstances. The apostle Paul and several of his companions are part of a shipload of prisoners being transported from Caesarea to stand trial in Rome; an imperial regiment centurion named Julius is responsible for them. The trip proves to be quite a harrowing one. First they encounter a wicked wind that necessitates a slight detour and change of ships. On the second ship they make slow headway again, encountering an even greater detour because of the winds. They lose a lot of time, and sailing becomes even more dangerous because the stormy sea season is upon them. After finally reaching a safe port, Paul warns the centurion Julius that the voyage is going to be a disastrous one if they do not stay and wait out the season. The centurion consults the ship's owner and captain and then apparently takes a vote; the majority decision is to sail on to Phoenix, where they figure they can winter well.[3]

As Paul predicted, the seemingly favorable south wind they set out with turns into a hurricane-force "northeaster" that hurls the ship off course. They nearly lose the lifeboat, risk running aground on sandbars, and take such a violent battering that they have to toss the ship's tackle overboard. After days and nights of sheer darkness, they give up all hope of survival.

Then an angel visits Paul one night and assures him that although the ship will be destroyed while running aground on some island, no lives will be lost. After a brief "I told you so," Paul tries to comfort the crew with this revelation (but let us be real: would *you* believe a guy talking about what an angel told him?). Fourteen days into the ordeal, Paul notices the ship's crew preparing to steal away in the lifeboat—a threat to everyone else's survival. He alerts Julius, who finally has a sense that Paul may know what he is talking about, and Julius has his soldiers cut the lifeboat free. A little while later they muster up the wherewithal to eat for the first time in two weeks and then further risk their survival by tossing all the grain overboard in an effort to lighten the ship.

The next morning, the weary travelers see a bay with a sandy beach on which they think they may be able to run aground. Alas, they are met by yet one more disastrous disappointment: before they get to the beach, the bow runs aground on a sandbar. Now the soldiers fear the prisoners will escape, and so they plan to kill them so they cannot swim away. However, Julius wants to spare Paul and counters with a lifesaving plan of his own. Julius' plan is a success and, as the angel promised, they all reach shore a bit beaten but alive.

So, amidst all the adventure and drama, did you take note of some different ways we chart uncharted territory? Did you empathize at all with the ship's crew and soldiers, so caught up in reaching their destination that they lost the ability to consider and assimilate relevant information and to make good judgments? Some of us do not travel well: we easily lose our composure and cool. Some of us even risk taking care of ourselves in tough times (refusing to eat and rest) and become reactionary rather than remaining proactive. Some of us are like Julius, caving in to popular opinion. Meanwhile Paul was disciplined and focused. He believed and did whatever it took to remain in constant connection with God, knowing that God's direction and assurances are always the best and the only reliable compass. In our terms, we might say that Paul knew the importance of _holding environments_ and had learned how to hold on to them, even in the midst of storms and turmoil.

HOLDING ENVIRONMENTS

But a holding environment is not only necessary during times of storms and turmoil. In many respects, it is the place from which the journey emerges. We will say a good bit more about this dynamic in the final chapter, but for now consider one more experience with a holding environment that has had a dramatic effect on a congregation not too unlike many in the United States.

I had the opportunity to meet with the leaders of this congregation's evangelism team about six months after my colleague, Martha Grace Reese, had first consulted with them. When Martha Grace first met with them, the leaders had recently assumed leadership, and she found them as I did: excited, enthusiastic, brimming with ideas, and ready to "get started." But instead of picking up on their ideas, she invited them to spend the next three months meeting weekly to intentionally pray for themselves, their pastors, the other people in the church, those not affiliated with a church, and anything else they thought to pray about. She also encouraged the pastor to help reign in any attempts to move on ideas until the three months had passed.

As you might imagine, the task was not an easy one, particularly for this team of driven, energized, creative, idea-filled folks; but they rose to the challenge and for three months did little more than pray, meet, pray, and share what they "heard" God saying to them. And, mercy, did God talk, and were they listening!

I met with them three months after they had begun implementing plans, and already they had mobilized the congregation to greet and follow up with all guests. This was a big deal and massive effort for that congregation, but one of the dilemmas the leadership shared with me was that they had too many helpers and were concerned folks might become discouraged or feel dishonored because the response had been so great and there were not yet enough guests! I encouraged them to keep praying and thought that the guests might come.

As you may have guessed: they have . . . and they have! Over the past year, attendance at all their programs and services has increased significantly, and the congregation has received more new members and had more baptisms (including adults) than in a long time. As a result, they are now anticipating a multimillion dollar capital campaign that will provide the needed space they once only contemplated. People in the know talk about what has happened as a result of a few folks gathering to pray and *listen*, and the discipline is spreading into other structures of the congregation.

One of the dangerous tactical mistakes we make in our congregations is impatience. While some churches are slow to move, others are like horses champing at the bit. We find ideas and move swiftly, often too swiftly. Our baskets are half empty (or half full) and we do not line up our ducks in the proverbial row. We go off with our guns half-cocked and with both barrels blazing.

PACING

Planning and follow-through are crucial, but a key piece in our plans has to be a provision for holding environments. We have to give ourselves permission, and be intentional about, finding oases along the transformational journey. This is particularly important when we encounter the wilderness. We have to be intentional about scheduling, or finding ways to discover those safe fertile sanctuaries, the oases, along the way so we can guard against any drive to get to our destination too quickly. It can be helpful to remember that it is, after all, God's promised land and it will be there when we arrive! We need those places of re-creation along the way where we can take stock and refresh ourselves.

I am reminded of the warrior Gideon and God's call for him to save Israel from the mighty, oppressive power of the Midianites. God's call starts with a general direction: "Go in this might of yours and deliver Israel out of Midian's hand."[4] But Gideon, even though he is taking this call seriously, does not jump in too hastily; he takes some time to make sure the message he is getting is really from God. First, he engages in a bit of worship, doing what he can to put God and who God is in the proper perspective to make sure that what he is hearing is coming from God and not from his own ego or wishful thinking.

Part of this task involves a little detour to tear down the altar to Baal and build one to the Lord God, a task that pits Gideon against his fellow Israelites and nearly costs Gideon his life.[5] But he perseveres, honing his character and leadership skills in so doing. In the meantime, the Midianites join forces with the Amalekites and other eastern peoples.[6] Gideon's assurance appears to waver. Just to make sure he and God are on the same page, Gideon spends another couple of days in discernment, tossing out a couple of fleeces.[7]

Now we might think Gideon is ready to head off into battle. But there are a few more details to work out. Gideon finds he has enlisted *too many* men (and he was worried he would not be able to put together a large enough army!), so he has to reduce the ranks not once but twice. From there Gideon moves his forces in to place; but even with an army certified by God, Gideon does not rush into battle. He waits, deals with encroaching fear,[9] and then worships some more.[10] *Then* he is finally ready to implement his plan and taste the sweetness of freedom.[11] Gideon knows the art of pacing.] *Timing*

I once coached a network of house churches and was intentional about each house church planning at least one mission project and one "evangelistic" effort per quarter. Each house church pastor had a planning calendar, and I worked with them to plan their outreach and evangelism as far in advance as possible. We then worked backward from those events to calendar details such as intercession, invitations, and other arrangements that needed to be made. I coupled this work with accountability that included checking in on the pastors' spiritual disciplines, the practices that deepen their relationship with God and allow them to better "hear" from God.

Month after month, I challenged the house church pastors to think about how each part of what they did contributed to the whole of what they and their congregations believed God was wanting them to be and do. Their journeys in no way looked the same, for they were as individual as the house churches and those leading them. But we might describe them figuratively as engaging processes of walking, running, treading lightly, pushing, resting, hiking uphill, and so on: always on the journey, always monitoring, always pacing.[12] We worked hard with our pastors to identify and create holding environments for them and, through them, for the house churches. We were intentional about the how's and when's for holding space for God and making allowances for being held by Jesus and the Holy Spirit. Sometimes that took more time than any of us would have liked, but we always found it worked best.

Though a stickler for planning and process, I am also reminded that we can get too bogged down in the details or fear of making mistakes. Mistakes are not always deadly, and we cannot allow ourselves to be immobilized by fear of making them. Indeed, we need to prepare for the worst, but hope—and pray—for the best. Getting bogged down is another challenge some of our congregations face. Err on the side of caution: be thorough, think through your plans and their implementation, test them with God (perhaps lay out a couple of fleeces of your own), retest and check in along the way, and remember to hold space for addressing and dealing with anxiety and fear. Indeed, Gideon offers a good model for us and reminds us how important composure is for surviving the transformational journey. Without it, we move too close to those time bombs of urgency and distraction, and we risk diversion or, worse yet, getting blown completely off the transformational road.

Notes

1. Ronald Heifetz and Marty Linsky, *Leadership on the Line: Staying Alive through the Dangers of Leading* (Boston: Harvard Business School Press, 2002) 120.

2. Ibid., 132.

3. Note that this is the only vote taken in the Bible (other than Paul's mention of putting Christians to death in Acts 26:10) and it is a disastrous one!

4. Judges 6:14a.

5. Judges 6:17–32.

6. Judges 6:33.

7. Judges 6:36–40.

8. Judges 6:15.

9. Judges 7:10–14

10. Judges 7:15.

11. For the full story of Gideon, read Judges 6–8.

12. Although I individually met monthly with each house church pastor, we also brought the house church pastors together each week for group training, check-in, care, and prayer.

STAY ON COURSE

It has been said that congregations are like ocean vessels heading toward a common destination.[1] They come in all shapes and sizes, each takes its own route, and each has its own particular purpose. Some are cruise ships, some are sailboats, some are fishing trawlers, some are tugs pushing barges, some are for search and rescue—you get the picture.

THE PRINCE'S CRUISE LINES

Many of us face the challenge that for a while we were on magnificent cruise ships with an assortment of options: smorgasbords of ministries for men and women; great halls with scrumptious buffets and choir floor-shows; rec rooms filled with activities and fun for youth and children; parlors for lounging and intimate gatherings; decks filled with parties and other fun events; and swimming pools full of newcomers ready to dive in to things. We attracted and could serve a wide variety of folks wanting a wide variety of services and entertainment. You could call us the Prince's Cruise Line.[2]

But today the Prince's Cruise Line presents us with two problems. The first is that it is an aging enterprise, and with that comes some serious safety risks that put the ship in danger of sinking. Many of our vessels have become old and rusty and have taken on leaks that are draining our revenues. Folks no longer automatically board our ship because of its denominational affiliation, and there is a lot of competition for the entertainment and other opportunities that were once exclusively ours. As such, there have been fewer and fewer passengers signing on, even for our exclusive excursions. Some of our folks have jumped ship, and we are concerned about whether or not we have enough staff to keep us afloat. Add to that the cash flow problems, the resultant downsizing, and the harsh reality that we are only a shadow of our former glory.

The second problem with the Prince's Cruise Line is that over the years it has helped cultivate a culture of service: but one of *being served* rather than of *serving*. On Prince's cruises you often hear, "I don't like that program, so I'm not going to support it"; or "The pastor's sermons just don't feed me"; or "We can't do that because I won't go"; or, worse yet, "I'll stop coming." Like the centurion Julius in Acts 27, a lot of churches base major decisions on the majority votes of "what *I* like" or have come to expect rather than on what God expects or might like.

During my early life as a Christian I once found myself in what would become a contentious church board meeting. The neighborhood in which that church was located had experienced White flight[3] a decade earlier and in as many years the congregation had gone from more than five hundred members to fewer than fifty. The congregation had begun growing under a new pastor's leadership, but with that growth came families that did not "look like us."

That ill-fated board meeting began with the requisite opening prayer and remarks, and then the pastor brought the first order of business before the board: two biracial families who had been visiting the church over the past twelve or so weeks were contemplating joining the church. In actuality, this was not a board issue, but the pastor knew the racial views of some of those in leadership and was hoping to diffuse and defuse potential negative reactions. His only perceived alternative was to have to go to the two families (who had been unchurched for years) and tell them, first, that the church would not likely welcome them and, second, that he feared for their safety. He could not bear what kind of message that would give the two families.

At the board meeting, the pastor began, "I want to let the board know we will likely be receiving two new families into membership in the next few weeks." At first the board heard the news expectantly (the last new members had joined a couple of years earlier when a sister church had closed its doors), but many of them—even though they were a congregation averaging less than seventy-five in worship—could not figure out who the potential new members were. The pastor mentioned the names of the couples and someone mentioned that they were "the two biracial families."

The lay leader spoke up first, "Are you asking us to take a vote on whether or not they can become members?"

Referring to page numbers and paragraphs, the pastor replied that the denomination's policy was not to vote on membership but, rather, to welcome everyone who professes Jesus as Savior and is baptized. It did not take long for the meeting to deteriorate, prompting a known Klansman to stand up and declare that it would be over his "dead body that any [fill-in-a-racial-epithet] joined" *his* church.

Concerns along this line continued for another minute or so before someone asked to be recognized by the chair, stood, and quietly said, "I thought this was *Jesus'* church." There was a moment of silence before the lay leader shot back, "It may be Jesus' church, but we pay the bills."

While this may be an extreme example, shots like those of the lay leader continue now, nearly twenty years later, in churches around the world. "I'll take my money away with me if you hire that person." "I'm afraid I can't get behind that program, so I think I'll have to start going to the church down the road." "Jesus' church? I help pay the bills. . . ." "I'll take my tithe!" Serve me . . . or else.

An earlier pastor at that church I just mentioned once explained to me that when our inner-city neighborhood began transitioning, the few remaining members of the congregation had come to huddle together within the church, seeking it almost as a refuge. The church's mission had become one of care to the "faithful holdouts" who remained. In many respects, those folks found themselves on a different ship than the Prince's Cruise Line they had boarded thirty, forty, fifty years earlier. Not only was that ship a ghost of its former glory, the new pastor was trying to convert it into a fishing trawler.

In the years since that board meeting I have talked to numerous folks who are coming to terms with the reality that they are no longer on the Prince's Cruise Line. Many are angry with the pastors who remind us that we have had to downsize and convert. Fishing is hard, often smelly, work. Few of us have learned how to fish and, quite honestly, we do not want to learn. Many of us are feeling seasick and are trying to get our bearings, holding on to anything we can find. You may see us as territorial as we hold on to our state rooms, our kitchens, our parlors, our Sunday school classrooms, our former positions of glory (which are often masked positions of privilege). We repeat the mantra, "I am a passenger, not some servant; the church is here to serve me." Sometimes we find ourselves spewing those mantras to anyone who will—or we think should—listen. Our attempts to assert our once privileged positions in the congregation are as much for the benefit of others as they are reminders to ourselves of who we are . . . of who we have been.

STROLLING DOWN MEMORY LANE

"My aunt was the first woman baptized in this congregation," a threatened older member once felt a need to tell me. A week later another long-timer came by my office to present his pedigree: he had had a distinguished military career, had been the mayor of the town, had chaired the deacons and nearly every committee in the congregation. I figured out later that he was not sharing his experience with an offer to use it for the building up of the church and/or God's realm; he was there to make sure I did not usurp his position or otherwise butt heads with him.

I have heard similar stories from across the country, and perhaps you have as well. "I was here when this church began." "I remember meeting in that old trailer that used to do double duty as our Sunday school building and sanctuary." "My father used to be the minister here." "My mother was the head of the women's organization." And . . . ? And maybe you are a bit like me and have spewed in spite of yourself when the seas got a little tumultuous.

Strolling down memory lane for the purposes of remembering both good and not-so-good times and stirring memories of God's work in our midst can be positive and helpful (and even hope-filling). I love looking at congregational histories and hearing stories from the mothers and fathers and sons and daughters of congregations. I love to see the smiles on their faces as they recount stories of triumph and courage. I have learned a lot about perseverance and endurance in tears and frowns. I hold on to the testimonies of God's work and the cherished reminders that God is still working in the lulls and storms. I have also come to seek clarity from early histories and memories, looking for clues and confirmations about why congregations were birthed, why God called them in to being.

Yet it is something else entirely to reminisce for the sake of posturing privilege. Engaging collective congregational recollection can be an important tool that allows us to consider and connect (often, *re*connect) to our congregation's overarching journey and purpose, particularly as we bring new generations on board. It is similar to sharing the family album and telling stories about this grandparent or that long-lost auntie.

But we have to be careful. I have a friend who enjoys looking at his wife's picture albums from her years before "them." Many of those albums include pictures of "her" four children and ex-husband. My friend does not mind the repeated requests from the children to look at the albums and even enjoys their stories of days gone by. He recognizes that these were happy parts of this part of his family's life, that they capture important moments, and that the recollections help him gain insight into who his family was, is, and is becoming.

Over the years, his wife has been able to establish a working relationship with her ex-husband, who left her for another woman and still lives near her parents' home in another part of the country. In fact, her ex has worked hard to remain a presence in her parents' lives, something her parents think is a good thing "for the sake of the children." My friend says that none of this bothers him, except on holidays when the ex-husband shows up and tries to create an atmosphere reminiscent of the way things "used to be."

Invariably, at some point during the holiday get-togethers the ex-husband starts the stroll down memory lane. It usually starts innocently enough when someone spills a drink or makes a passing comment to which someone responds, "Do you remember when. . . ?" My friend notes that the memories start strolling from there and nearly everyone gets caught up in the laughter and fond memories: everyone, that is, but my friend. Rather, he becomes an innocent observer who is at risk of being left out from yet one more memory-making moment.

The first problem here may be obvious. My friend is left out because his wife and her family get so caught up with peering into the windows of their memories that they forget he cannot see in too because he has never been on that road. Collective reminiscing can be a good tool for building cohesion, but it can also invite exclusion.

The other problem lies with the intent of the ex-husband. He is not as innocent as some might like to think; *his* parents have even mentioned that they think he knows what a mistake he made in leaving "his family." In fact, my friend has only recently begun to recognize the way the ex-husband uses (often inspires) the memory strolls to intimate a privilege he once had with the wife. His motives are not so pure; underneath all the reminiscing lies a slight suggestion that things could be better than they remember . . . if only he might be allowed to reassume his former position in the family!

Fortunately, my friend has a good relationship with his wife and they have been able to discuss these dynamics and his concerns. They try to be more conscious about how their family's memories can stroll along, and they are trying to frame them in the light of the family's bigger journey. Memories are part of where we have been that inform and shape where we are, and they can either remain in the past or expand daily to help inform and shape our futures . . . and the futures of our children and the families they will one day have.

VALUES, MISSION, AND VISION

It takes a lot of work and intentionality, but my friend and his wife are committed to that "bigger journey." To that end, they regularly work to remember three significant commitments they made to one another at the beginning of their relationship, namely:

1. To be open and honest.

2. To continually do the work necessary to have a healthy marriage so they could be a unified partnership that would come to have a positive influence not only on their children, but on the world as well.

3. To raise the children in as safe and loving an environment as possible that would allow the children to be relatively healthy adults who contribute to, rather than take away from, others.

In one sense, what my friend and his wife have committed to are *values*, a *mission*, and a *vision*. They value openness and honesty and know that the strength of their vision and mission depends on their ability to live these at all times. Their mission (why they exist as a couple) is to have a positive influence on the world. Their vision (how they are living out that mission in the now) is to raise children who will one day also positively influence the world.

Of course, having a happy marriage is something they value, but they realize that marriage is not always happy, that there are tough times. They know that if they focus too much on happiness, they may lose sight of the influence they can have. Likewise, there are days they would like to "throw it all away," sell the house, and head off to some distant foreign-mission shore, but that is not a workable possibility for them at this point. Their children need to be in continental proximity to the father, and they do not think it would be in their best interest (either the children's or the family's as a whole) to pursue the measures that might let them do it. If nothing else, it would be a detour that would add unnecessary stressors, would detract from their goal to significantly influence the world, and could possibly jeopardize the children's safety and future potential to be world contributors rather than consumers.

As long as they are able to remain focused on their values, mission, and vision, my friend and his wife are able to cope with the bouts of depression and poor decisions that plague their family from time to time. There have been times they were ready to give in and give up; but so far they have always been able to refocus and recover.

All this takes a lot of energy, but they find that their energy is renewed and multiplied every time they remember why they became a couple in the first place and reminisce about the times when their marriage "works" and the ways in which they have managed, even when it has not worked so well. They need that energy and focus because they know that not only their marriage but the lives of their children and others they know are affected by their ability to be open, honest, and a healthy couple of influence.

My friend has mentioned that their values, mission, and vision are like lighthouses that help him and his wife navigate their marriage and warn them of danger. When things seem to be rocky or stormy, they tend to do check-ins about what they are feeling, where the feelings are coming from, and whether or not they have arrived in situations they might have been better to avoid. The National Park Service notes that

> the message of the lighthouse might be—STAY AWAY, DANGER, BEWARE, or COME THIS WAY. Every lighthouse tells the mariner, "This is exactly where you are.[5]

My friend and his wife have learned over the years that they are in for a stormy and potentially dangerous ride when they ignore or neglect the light shed by their values, mission, and vision.

Values, mission, and vision are no less important for churches. Much has been written about the need for congregations to know, own, and live their "mission, vision, and values.[6] When consulting with congregations, I start with two basic questions: (1) "Do you have a mission statement?" and (2) "What is your vision?"

I used to be heartened by the number of pastors who would say, "Yes, we have a mission statement." But then I realized how few could tell me what their mission or vision was without having to search their files for a copy: often because the statements were several paragraphs long and, just as often, because the process they had engaged to develop the statements was in some way divisive and they had filed the statements away with the hope that the painful memories would go away with them.

Simply put, the *mission* of a church answers the question as to why God has called that particular congregation into being. The easiest way to find this is to go back to the congregation's early board minutes, reports, and newsletters to look for why the founding mothers and fathers risked time, talent, and treasure to start a new church when and where they did. The *vision* articulates how the congregation is living into that mission today: it describes what the congregation is spending time, talent, and treasure to accomplish. *Values* define what the congregation is willing to risk to be faithful to God's mission and vision for this particular congregation.

FROM COMPETITION TO CLARITY

Knowing, owning, living, and continuously remembering our mission, vision, and values are more important for the transformational journey than we might possible imagine. First, knowing, owning, and living our mission, vision, and values are crucial for setting, clarifying, and staying on course. For years, many of us have been steering our churches with a "y'all come" strategy. "Y'all come," no matter who you are or what you are looking for. "Y'all come," as long as you act like us, particularly during the worship services. "Y'all come," as long as you do not rock the boat too much. In our quests for numbers, cash flow, and (providing for the "benefit of the doubt") reaching people because the church has something to offer, we have done a lot of bending over backwards and dust-kicking to cloud the reality that it is next to impossible to be everything to everyone.

As a result, our churches are filled with a lot of competing values and views. It is no wonder our board meetings can be contentious: all the board members are fighting for—okay, "loudly disagreeing about"—what they believe is right or in their best interest. Too many churches are wrestling over what exactly is in the church's best interest. I have heard such church striving summarized as a small group of sailors who have made their way into the pilot house and are grasping for the wheel as they argue with the captain and navigational crew about how and where to steer the ship.

Can you imagine that happening on a ship? That would be mutiny! But it is happening over and over again in our congregations; and with it come foggier focus, drained energy, loss of enthusiasm, and lost opportunities. When our mission, vision, and values are clear, the questions become:[7]

- ◆ "How does this enhance, embody, and/or further our reason for being?"

- ◆ "Who has God provided to facilitate and work in this endeavor?"

- ◆ "How will we fund it?"[8]

The service attitude (that of being served as opposed to having a servant attitude) we have acquired and perpetuate has clouded our memories, and too often we forget to ask, "What is it, God, that you want? What is right with you?"

Another benefit to being clear about our course is that one of the greatest gifts we can give guests and church seekers who make their way to our churches is counsel and direction about where they might best worship and serve God. I have helped charismatic folks find churches with good, solid ministries and charismatic worship. I have recommended other congregations to families with young children when I have served congregations with no viable children's ministries. Effective churches everywhere intentionally sit with potential members to help them both explore the ship they have boarded and to determine whether or not they want to stay on this particular vessel. One church I have known would close their conversations with potential members with the following invitation:

> You basically have three choices at this point. (1) If you like what you have seen, have heard, and are experiencing, you can join us. (2) If you are not yet sure, you can hang around here for as long as you like, but we would like to reserve the right to check in with you from time to time. And (3) if you are not sure this is the church for you, let's talk more and see what church in the area might be a better fit.

Being clear about our mission, vision, and values allows us to be lighthouses and places of direction for those who are reeling from the storms that brought them to us in the first place.

Clarity about our mission, vision, and values is also crucial for getting our congregations back on course. We have already mentioned that the winds of change have knocked many of us off course and we have found ourselves pulling into ports aboard ships that look nothing like the ones on which we departed!

DISCOVERY VERSUS DEVELOPMENT

As we consider mission, vision, and values work, it can be helpful to talk in terms of *discovery* (or *recovery*) rather than considering the process as one of *development*. Just as God has created each of us uniquely, God has uniquely called each congregation into being to live in, out, and through the Great Commandments and Great Commission. Many of our congregations have become far removed from the unique purposes for which God created us, from those to whom God has sent us to serve, and from how God wants us to live out that service. We have become so wrapped up with being passengers that we have forgotten that we are crew members first and that it is our work and invitations that set the tables; produce the floor-shows; fill the rec rooms, decks, and parlors; sponsor the parties and events; and see to it that the swimming pools are always full. I say "forgotten" because somewhere in the early days of each congregation we knew our purpose and we were enthused about our mission and vision.

Consultant George Bullard has done a bit of work identifying and explaining the life cycles of congregations. George notes that there are four aspects in congregational life:

1. Vision (which encompasses vision, mission, purpose, core values, and leadership)

2. Relationships (which comprises relationships, experience, and discipleship)

3. Programs (comprising program, events, ministries, services, and activities)

4. Management (including management, accountability, systems, and resources).[9]

Congregations are conceived and brought into being around the first aspect: with vision, mission, purpose, values, and leadership. The people who birth the congregation are also in relationship; are doing ministry, service, and/or activities together; have a certain sense of accountability to one another; and have a enough management systems in place to make sure things can get done. But vision is what guides them.

Soon relationships become as important and as prominent a driving factor as vision. People are excited about the vision, want others to be part of it, and are enthusiastic about the relationships they are building.

This continues until there are enough people that programming needs to become more systematized (see Figure 1. George Bullard's Congregational Life Cycle). Relationships are still important, but the organization foci shift from vision and relationships to vision and programming. As the congregation matures, it begins to find a balance between vision, programming, and relationships; management is still necessary and evident, but it is not as large a focus as the first three until the congregation reaches a certain level of maturity. At that stage, vision, relationships, programs, and management come into their fullness, equally weighted and balanced.

Figure 1. George Bullard's Congregational Life Cycle[10]

LIFE STAGE	DOMINANT ASPECTS			
BIRTH	VISION	relationships	programs	management
INFANCY	VISION	RELATIONSHIPS	programs	management
CHILDHOOD	VISION	relationships	PROGRAMS	management
ADOLESCENCE	VISION	RELATIONSHIPS	PROGRAMS	management
ADULTHOOD	VISION	RELATIONSHIPS	PROGRAMS	MANAGEMENT
MATURITY	vision	RELATIONSHIPS	PROGRAMS	MANAGEMENT
EMPTY NEST	vision	RELATIONSHIPS	programs	MANAGEMENT
RETIREMENT	vision	relationships	PROGRAMS	MANAGEMENT
OLD AGE	vision	relationships	programs	MANAGEMENT
DEATH	—	—	—	management

A congregation's arrival at the "maturity" stage of life is marked by a decreased emphasis on vision. This usually happens about the time the founding generation begins to pass the baton to the next generation, which often has no articulated sense of the founding vision. The congregation is now at risk of decline. If the vision is not recaptured and a balance reclaimed, the congregation will next likely see their programs fade away, leaving them with relationships and management. As the cycle continues, relationships will diminish to the extent that programs will appear to be as important as management; however, management will eventually dominate. Death is delineated by the appearance of only management; the vision, relationships, and programs will have all passed away.

Do you see in George's work how natural it can be to drift away from our reasons for being on the church scene in the first place? I think of how many journeys are put on hiatus or are otherwise thwarted because of circumstances that can come our way: debilitating diseases, economic downturns, births and deaths, bad choices, good choices that turned out to be not so good after all. Over the years and with a propensity to be blown about by this wind or that, it is easy to lose sight of what course we are on, particularly when the lighthouse lights have become dim or fogged over.

SEND OUT YOUR LIGHT

Without the light of our lighthouses we can easily get confused and lost, wandering aimlessly for years. Our ability to make good, on-course decisions becomes compromised. A lot of us are even understandably confused about what ship we are on because our captains and crew have not checked on the light bulbs. Others of us have waded into the Sea of Dissatisfaction because we have found ourselves resting in a different port than we anticipated, no doubt because our ships changed routes somewhere in midroute: partly because those winds of change blew steadily while we were sleeping (or partying), partly because there have been so many midcourse corrections for long enough that our journeys shifted much more significantly than anyone realized along the way. But now that we are seasick, lost, longing for a familiar port, or in need of provisions, we know something is wrong.

If we will allow our mission, vision, and values to be like the bright light that emanates from the lighthouse and if we can catch sight of the light, reclaim our original mission, and get back on course, our futures can become much brighter and clearer. Most of us know that, but not enough of us are taking it to heart.

I believe it was Bill Easum who taught me that mission and vision have to be recast continuously. We need look no further than Moses' first hours out of Egypt for a prime example of what we are talking about here: "Excuse me, Moses, but I thought we were going into the promised land. We don't like the desert!"[11]

Indeed, the Israelites were only three days away from their incredible escape from Egypt when Moses had yet another crisis on his hands.[12] The Israelites had seen their leader Moses do miraculous signs and wonders. They had seen Moses' words come true. They had themselves experienced the parting of the great Red Sea that allowed them to escape to the other side while it closed and drowned Pharaoh's soldiers who had been pursuing them.

But all that was three days ago. Now they are in the Desert of Shur and they have not been able to find any water, and when they get to Marah, they find that the water is bitter and undrinkable. "So, Moses, here we are! What are we supposed to drink?"[13]

God intervenes yet again here and promises the Israelites that if they will stay on track, listen carefully to the voice of God, do what is right in God's eyes, and pay attention, God will protect them. Exodus 15:27 says, "Then they came to Elim, where there were twelve springs of water and seventy palm trees, and they camped there by the water."

Experience and myriad stories tell us that God is still in the miracle and protection business. I live by the standard, "Be faithful with the little and God will give you more; be faithful with the more and God will entrust you with even more than that." It boils down to trust and faithfulness, though: trusting that God will be faithful while being faithful with the mission and vision God has entrusted to you.

I often wish that our missions, visions, and values were equipped with foghorns that blast in the storms and fog. Perhaps, though, we can build in foghorns by first getting clear about our missions, visions, and values and then setting up practices that will remind us of them along the way: designing our board meeting agendas around our mission, vision, and values; planning and evaluating *all* our ministries and programs based on whether or not they embody and enhance our mission, vision, and values; regularly measuring paid and volunteer staff effectiveness by our (yes, say it with me) mission, vision, and values. Then, even in the dark times when we are likely to slip into survival mode, we will have built-in lighthouses to remind us of where we are going, to warn us that we are in treacherous waters, and to redirect us as necessary.

It is dangerous enough to steer through storms and fog; why on earth do we want to do that alone, particularly when the waves are crashing us about and folks are fighting for the wheel? When left to our own devices, our panicked, reactive efforts can be like headlights in the fog that do little more than bounce back and can potentially blind us and make things tougher to see. We need lighthouses and foghorns to help us make it through without serious injury.

Whether our journeys take us by land or air or sea, the rigors and storms—natural and unnatural—are untold. We have to be prepared to stay on course. We not only have to know up front what kind of vessel we are on, we need the constant reminders so we do not become confused or discouraged and jump overboard.

There is a lot that can distract us . . . and that gets multiplied by each of us in the congregation. I typically wear contact lenses and regularly experience what the commercials call grit. All I know is that it feels like there is a piece of gravel between my eye and the contact lens. It is uncomfortable and it fools with my eyesight (not good when you have to drive), and it tends to draw my attention away from matters at hand. Churches experience this phenomenon, too. Whether our journey is transformation or merely faithfulness to living as Jesus calls and teaches, we have to have and maintain clarity. One of the foundational ways we do this is by knowing, owning, and living our congregational mission, vision, and values.

Although my optometrist thinks I can do perfectly well with a contact lens prescription, I find myself regularly falling back on the basics of eyesight correction: my glasses. There is something refreshing about slipping contacts out at the end of a long day and remembering how clear one's sight can be when we go back to those basics. And I must confess I wonder sometimes why I even wear the contacts, remembering that eye correction is about clear focus rather than cosmetic appeal.

Let Your Light Shine

It is the same with the church. There has been a move over the past few years to establish ministries or offer events or programs that will attract others or that make us feel more attractive. Often those "things" have little or nothing to do with what it means to do or be church today. As we discussed in chapter 3, certain programs and activities and plans are often more fitting for another congregation than for ours. Sometimes our plans serve more as foggy windows onto memory lane or are a vain attempt to save our state rooms. In these cases, we risk losing focus and direction *and* our journey, God's journey, for the congregation.

We have to keep our focus, be prepared to remember the specific role our congregation plays in the community of faith, in the community beyond our doors, and in the realm of God. Being clear and owning our mission, vision, and values allows us to do that in a way nothing else can provide.

Jesus was so focused on his mission and vision that he repeatedly risked angering the people who had the power to hold life and death over his head (or so they thought). That clarity gave him the courage to call one of his closest friends and best students "Satan." That clarity gave him the strength and stamina to stay on the torturous path that led to Jerusalem and one of the most excruciating deaths ever recorded. Jesus knew why he had been birthed into a human body and what he had to accomplish. Nothing and no one—not even himself—got in the way. His journey was fraught with a number of time bombs that could have thwarted his purpose, but his mission and vision shed light onto the path and defused the explosions that might have destroyed God's plan.

The transformational journey is not only about us; it is about those who need the church both today and in the tomorrows to come. To avoid and defuse our congregational time bombs, we must know, own, and live into and out of our mission, vision, and values. We must allow them to serve as lighthouses and fog horns that keep us on course. Our very lives, as well as the lives of those who are depending on us, are at stake. Keep your eyes and ears open so *your* light may shine in the dark, dreary, storms of this world.

Programs are to meet needs of people and fulfill the mission of the church.

Notes

1. I first heard this analogy from Kurt Oheim, founding pastor of Pinnacle, a congregation in Amarillo, Texas (at http://www.sayingyes.com).

2. As in the Prince of Peace.

3. White flight describes the exodus of Caucasians from neighborhoods when people of color begin to move in.

4. I am not telling stories here, merely details that will prove important in a moment.

5. National Park Service, "Apostle Islands: Lighthouse Curriculum, Part A," http://www.nps.gov/apis/forkids.

6. I cannot recommend highly enough the prolific work of Bill Easum and Tom Bandy (see easumbandy.org), particularly Tom's "trilogy": *Kicking Habits Upgrade: Welcome Relief for Addicted Churches* (Nashville: Abingdon Press, 2000); *Coming Clean: The Study Guide to Kicking Habits* (Nashville: Abingdon Press, 2001); and *Facing Reality: A Tool for Congregational Mission Assessment* (Nashville: Abingdon Press, 2001). Tom's approach is one of the most grounded, holistic approaches for mission, vision, and value discovery and ownership that draws on discerning God's intentions for the congregation within the context of where the congregation has been, is, and will be historically, demographically, systemically, missionally, and influentially.

7. These are basic "permission-giving" questions as modified from teachings by Bill Easum.

8. Note, this third question is *not*, "Will we fund it?"!

9. George Bullard, *Life Cycle of a Congregation Model* (Cary, NC: Lake Hickory Learning Communities, 2000).

10. This is an adaptation of George's much more detailed graph.

11. See Exodus, particularly chapters 1–18, for more background.

12. Exodus 15:22.

13. Exodus 15:24.

7

PLAY TOGETHER TO STAY TOGETHER

I had been pastoring for a little while in the great Pacific Northwest before I realized how much I missed Jell-O salad. Coming out of churches in Georgia and Kansas, I have been the consumer of some of the greatest Jell-O salads ever, and some of my colleagues in Washington suggested I might be one of those rare pastors who actually looks forward to Jell-O salad . . . just about *any* kind of Jell-O salad as long as it's sugar-free.

I realized that my missing Jell-O salad was in part because the congregations I had been serving were not accustomed to covered-dish dinners. In fact, get-togethers for fun and games were few and far between, and I realized I was missing the fun fellowships more than the Jell-O salad, and that there is a connection between playing and staying together. You know the adage, "the family that prays together, stays together." It goes for families, for couples, and, yes, for churches; and playing is almost as important as prayer.

The business of church can be pretty intense and invasive these days; church business is hard, and it can be messy. There is a lot of division in a lot of churches. We take ourselves seriously, sometimes too seriously. From time to time we need environments where we can step outside ourselves, be human, smile, and have some fun.

PLAY IS NOT JUST FOR CHILDREN

Many of us know the importance of child's play for motor, mental, and social development; but many of us don't realize the importance of play for adults. The stress and wellness specialists at Whole Person's Associates note that when

> we deny our childlike natures, we reflect a still widely held societal belief that play is "children's work," optional and frivolous, "not real," and something people are allowed to do only after all their work is done.[1]

The renowned play therapist Charles Schaeffer has found that "we are never more fully alive, more completely ourselves, or more deeply engrossed in anything than when we are playing."[2] Indeed, we know today that play can relieve tension and stress, increase happiness, and otherwise lead to more balanced lives and living.[3] In fact, psychotherapist William Glasser holds that humans are genetically driven by five basic needs: survival, love and belonging, power, freedom, and fun.[4] Pediatrician turned noted psychoanalytic theorist D. W. Winnicott observed that "[c]ultural experience begins with creative living first manifested as play."[5] As such, play is a basic and essential part of human need and development!

When it comes to play as an environment for holding transformation, Hara Estroff Marano notes that play "appears to allow our brains to exercise their very flexibility, to maintain and even perhaps renew the neural connections that embody our human potential to adapt, to meet any possible set of environmental conditions."[6]

In other words, play helps us meet the challenges that come our way!

PLAY AND THE PEOPLE IN OUR MIDST

Congregational play helps us meet those transformational challenges in a variety of ways. For instance, playing tells us a lot about the people in our midst. I remember an elder coming up to me the day after a congregation's first party-for-the-sake-of-playing event in years. He noted that until the evening before he had never fully realized how competitive one of his long-time friends was . . . a family friend for eighteen years with whom he had been cochairing a key ministry: "Did you see how he was jumping up there answering questions for the team when we were playing that game?" the elder asked. "I never realized how aggressive he can be!" Yes, play can be telling.

Some of us are competitive and need to win. Some of us are passive. Some of us are uncomfortable with smiling. Some of us lack social knowhow. Others of us lack patience . . . or grace. Still others of us never got over our playground bullying. Playing goes a long way to help us see ourselves and our brothers and sisters as real.

More than that, though, play has the ability to effect healthy interactions among people to the extent that cooperation, trust, joint collaboration, bonding, and significant levels of personal interaction can increase and improve. It is amazing what can happen when two adversaries at a board meeting have to play on the same team, or when we see the person we've perceived as the grumpiest Gus crack a smile (no matter how small).

PLAY AS AN OPPORTUNITY TO PLAY BEYOND OURSELVES

Play can shed light not only on those in our midst; it can tell us a little more about ourselves. One summer I had the pleasure of watching a middle-aged man "playing" with kites on the beach. He first caught my attention because he was down at the edge of the cold surf with a moderately large dark purple kite. The first time I saw him, he was holding this purple kite just over his head, but then I saw him bend over from the waist and pull the kite down until he was holding it out horizontally from his body. It looked a little odd at first, but then I noticed the wind caught the kite and began to swing the kite—and the man—around in a circle. Every few moments, the wind would whip the kite up into the air, with the man hanging on tightly; and the man would fight downward against the wind until the kite was again horizontal and he could swing around and around in circles.

Since I do not get to see many middle-age adults having so much uninhibited fun, I could not help but look around for signs of the man's family, thinking he might be dancing with this kite for his children's benefit. But all I could find was one empty lounge chair with two kites laying next to it in the sand and another kite attached and sailing high above it. Over the course of a week, I would pass this man on the beach, always by himself. Well, not exactly by himself: he had his kites and was always having an obviously good time. Somewhere along the line this man had learned what was fun to him and made a point of getting away to let his hair down, let his belly hang out, and dance in the wind with his kite-partner. I still smile today at that image. Oh, that all of us might be able to get away and experience such uninhibited self-discovery.

Hara Estroff Marano tells us, "Play is an exercise in self-definition; it reveals what we choose to do, not what we have to do. We not only play because we are. We play the way we are. And the ways we could be. Play is our free connection to pure possibility.[8]

Adult play, like play in children, provides us with opportunities to step out of the roles with which we have been identified, or with which we identify ourselves. Some of us take ourselves much too seriously and need to experiment with some different roles: for instance, people who can run a church and have fun as well!

When transformational journeys get rough, it is common for folks to "get tough" and steel themselves for the rough work that continually confronts us. Sometimes we barely smile, partly because we find little about which to smile, partly because we are afraid to let our guard down. Play times can provide much needed relief, as well as a safe place to step out of our imposed roles. And just as it is important for children to see the significant adults in their lives playing, it is important for congregants to see the pastor and board chair and other leaders playing and having fun. On one hand, it communicates our humanity; on another hand, it is extremely good modeling.

PLAY FOR PROBLEM SOLVING

Play also allows us to try out problem-solving skills in ways we have perhaps not explored. Simulation games (perhaps a modified version of *Sim City*) can help us think in parallel terms about our journey and the journeys we are playing out with our teammates. Playing team-based games in our congregations can reveal problem-solvers and solutions we never knew were there.

But there is more to this problem-solving aspect than meets the eye. We in North America seem to be conditioned to juxtapose "play" and "learning." We tell our children they can "go out and play" after they "finish their homework." We have "book work time" and "play time" at school; when we do not complete our assignments, we are not allowed to "play." But studies document the importance of incorporating play into learning and the value of teaching with, or through, play.[9]

In some way, play is actually able to trigger something in our brains that promotes learning and creativity.[10] We can see that creative aspect particularly in children's play. While we may look into the dining room and see a table that seats six, children can look at that same table and see a prison (chairs make good barred windows), a tent (when there's a table cloth available), a bakery kitchen or store counter, or even a huge indoor swing (as in the case of our three youngest children when we had a hanging table many years ago). In fact, one of the great outcries of recent years is that in our attempts to give our children the world, we have stopped providing them with simple items like empty boxes, pieces of material, and old articles of clothing that require them to use their imaginations.

Comedian Drew Cary's syndicated show *Whose Line Is It Anyway?* offers an adult twist to the "let's pretend" of childhood, and he has inspired a new generation of adults with games that call on us to think creatively. One of those games places people in teams of two and gives each a prop; the teams then take turns coming up with imaginative uses for their props. I have played this game several times with ministers and we laugh hilariously every time—even those of us who are not prone to laughter. I have also watched this game transform a group from one that was disjointed with members who had been yelling at one another over the course of several days into one that was relatively cohesive and eventually capable of working together.

Beyond the fun and games, Dutch studies have also shown that play makes us more cognitively capable.[11] We know that play aids in the development of understanding and personalized, reflective learning; and it is crucial for those utilizing higher-order thinking and thought processes that draw on a great deal of engagement.[12] Folks like Marano hold that "play is not an activity, it is an attitude."[13] In many respects it is a frame of mind that allows our neurotransmitters to work to solve problems.

As we intimated earlier, most adults know the rule about children playing together: never get involved in their arguments because they will resolve them long before we parents resolve the differences that arise between us when intervening on our children's behalf. I cannot help but wonder if children's play allows them to quickly solve and resolve their problems and move on. At the risk of sounding trite, there seems to be some truth in the words spoken by Captain James T. Kirk in one of the original *Star Trek* episodes: "The more complex the mind, the greater the need for the simplicity of play."[14] Play, particularly games that challenge us to solve "problems" collaboratively, can inspire and remind us that there are often options we may not readily see. In addition, the playing of those games can literally and figuratively put us in the "right frame of mind" for thinking and engaging adaptive challenges at a deeper level than we otherwise can!

PLAY AS PRACTICE

Another fascinating aspect of play that links it to the transformational journey comes to us through work by Brian Sutton-Smith, an anthropologist and the dean of Play Studies at the University of Pennsylvania. Sutton-Smith points out that play is actually fantasy, but that it is framed in reality; hence, "everything you do [in play] is real."[15] Play allows us to "play out," if you will, our anxieties and fear. In fact, play studies show

> that all developed forms of play typically include representations of the ancient emotions of anger, shock, fear, disgust, and sadness. . . . In fact, these emotions usually provide the major scenarios for the play. Thus anger is represented through attack in all play contests, fear is represented through physical risk taking, shock is represented in teasing and hazing play forms, disgust manifests itself in gross humor and profanity, and sadness by the inebriation inherent in many festivals.[16]

As such, play can be helpful in bringing buried emotions to the surface, as well as the thoughts and tongue-bitten words of our "polite, nice" brothers and sisters in Christ who have been conditioned to never say a disparaging word.

Sutton-Smith hopes that his research will better link play with its physical and psychological effects. He points out that play can actually simulate an anxiety attack without the endocrine and adrenaline responses.[17] Marano observes that these simulations actually allow us to experiment with, and explore, feelings we may otherwise keep dormant. In effect, play can provide a safe place where we can, for a change, be in charge of the circumstances. Play, in this respect, can allow congregations not only to acknowledge anxiety and fears but also to allow space for us to express them, albeit perhaps not verbally. Play can become a place for us to practice feeling and working through our feelings, rather than continually repressing and/or acting them out.

OTHER BENEFITS OF PLAY

Of course, there are a number of other benefits to play, all supported by numerous studies (for those of us who have not been fortunate to enjoy enough play to experience them for ourselves). Adults—and children—who play are happier and healthier. Play releases anxiety and stress. It can teach and improve communication skills, coping abilities, and life skills.[18] Bruce Williamson reminds us that play helps engender trust, personal sharing, cooperation, teamwork, and group bonding. He also notes that when integrated into seminars and workshops, it can help overcome nervousness so that participants can engage more fully and communicate more easily with others.[19] It is capable of activating (reactivating?) a sense of discovery and wonder. Play also stimulates our memories and reasoning capacities; and people who play tend to be more optimistic about the future.[20] Sutton-Smith has been quoted repeatedly as saying, "The opposite of play isn't work. It's depression. To play is to act out and be willful, exultant and committed, as if one is assured of one's prospects."

PLAY AS A GIFT WE CAN GIVE

Play truly is a gift to us as congregations as we travel along the transformational journey; it is a key holding environment for the emotional turmoil, time bombs, and thought-blocks we will no doubt encounter. More than that, though, reclaiming fun and play—and teaching and modeling them—is one of the greatest gifts we can give to ourselves and those with whom we are journeying. What a gift to live a life that is better balanced; to be happier and more resilient; to be optimistic, productive, and more effective not only in our congregational contexts but in our personal and professional lives as well.

Not all of us have had happy childhoods; indeed, many of us have had our childhoods tragically interrupted. Imagine what a gift play can be for an adult who has never had the opportunity to play . . . or for one reason or another has never learned, or has forgotten, how to play. Jesus tells us that unless we "change and become like children" we cannot enter the realm of heaven.[21] What a gift to offer a tool for finding and claiming our childlikeness!

At the other end of the life spectrum, studies are now showing that adults who play tend to live longer than those who do not play.[22] Many of our congregations in survival mode are marked by an aging membership. As we have mentioned several times, play helps to keep our minds sharp; it will help us stay engaged, vibrant, and vital: not only in the church but in our families and beyond. Unfortunately, though, as we age many of us lose lifelong friends and find ourselves otherwise removed from places to play (even with the rise of senior centers that offer an abundance of activities). Play is one of the kindest gifts we can give to those who will benefit greatly from fun, smile-inducing, thought-producing play.

PLAYING TOGETHER AS BELIEVERS

In Acts 2:42–47 we read that the believers

> devoted themselves to the apostles' teaching and fellowship, to the breaking of bread and the prayer. Awe came upon everyone, because many wonders and signs were being done by the apostles. All who believed were together and had all things in common; they would sell their possessions and goods and distribute the proceeds, as anyone had need. Day by day, as they spent much time together in the temple, they broke bread at home and ate their food with glad and generous hearts.

At times congregations fail to fellowship because they would rather spend as little time together as possible. It is amazing the stories we pastors get to hear and it is sad how many times those stories reveal that congregations are more full of acquaintances (or even enemies) than friends. Other than loving God, is there anything more important than loving others and having some fun?[23]

I believe I have already said that I know full well what it is to be the recipient of poison-pen letters. I know how hard it is to stand in front of a congregation and preach when you have families stationed around the sanctuary, positioned where everyone can see them sitting with their arms folded and scowling (or picking up their novels and reading them when the sermon begins). I know how hard it is to walk into a women's study where the matriarch and several of her cronies turn their back on you and later uninvite you from returning.

We spoke earlier about the capacity of younger children to quickly make up and move on. Obviously, most of us lose that childlike ability to move on as we grow older. While the Bible never says "forgive and forget," it does tell us to forgive . . . and to figure out how to be unified in purpose. When I meet with couples having relationship difficulties, I ask them, "Do you want to be in relationship with one another? Are you willing to address the past, but not dwell in it?" Basically, the question is, "Are you willing to move on?" Play does not make everything better or "right," but it can help us move on, and it broadens our chances for figuring out how to do that. We need to reclaim glad and generous hearts, and play can help.

How to Play

Know that introducing play is not always well or widely received. Start slowly: at first try scheduling something like a game night every six months or so. You may also have to be a bit surreptitious about it. On the shelves of my office you will find a variety of puppets, hats and ears, and other sorts of "toys." I have been known to hop down the center aisle of a worship service with bunny ears on to announce upcoming Easter events. I will grant you that some have viewed that as heretical when done in my preaching robe and stoles, but it did get a lot of folks smiling

99

(and they remembered that announcement!). I also hope to long remember the smiles of tired, overworked, high-powered business men and women setting up for too early worship services after I showed up at the back of the sanctuary wearing Max the dog's ears and reindeer antler from *The Grinch Who Stole Christmas.* Yes, they shook their heads, but then they broke out in smiles and giggles and became open to God in much more real and present ways. I have also found those big "walking" birds you can buy at fairs to be good for bringing smiles to those who need them—including ourselves.[24]

For a cheap, fun dinner with your executive committee, go to a fast food restaurant that has a kids' meal with Legos®. Eat the meals (you may have to order a few extra burgers or side salads) and award gold stars for perseverance (to those who finish last) and creativity (for those who build something that in no way resembles what they were "supposed to be" building). One pastor I know bought three small stuffed mice to regularly bring to board meetings after the board members had read *Who Moved My Cheese?*[25] Whenever someone appeared to be reactive rather than proactive, a mouse could be seen flying across the table. After a while, board members would pick up one of the mice and *hold* it up as a way of acknowledging their own concerns, anxieties, and fears. Those silly mice—seen mostly as stupid at first—became a relatively safe place for holding people's emotions.

Am I incredibly creative? Not really. Am I a puppeteer? No way. Am I an actress? Again, no: I suffer horrid stage fright. But somewhere along the line I was given the gift of fun and a childlike spirit. I want to encourage you to take that gift and claim it for yourself—and for your congregation—now, sooner than too late.

Pastor Jim Harnish reminds us that many congregations are already filled with critics who continually taunt us into playing *their* game. He notes that when he "tried to play by their terms or outmaneuver them, [he] always lost."[26] If you are in a transformational congregation, game playing is likely a series of time bombs that are already ticking all around you. We have a choice about the kind of games we are going to play in our congregations. Perhaps healthy, appropriate play is one more gift we can give to the critical and mean of spirit . . . a way to call them on their games, offer to exchange their bombs and poisoned pens for water cannons, and invite them to join us in something that will benefit them personally, professionally, and congregationally . . . not to mention beyond.

As we close this chapter, I want to invite you to ponder how play can help your congregation to live longer . . . to thrive . . . to survive the transformational journey. After all, what have you to lose? You might even have a little fun along the way!

Notes

1. Bruce Williamson, "Introduction," in *Playful Activities For Powerful Presentations*, Whole Person Associates, 1993, http://www.wholeperson.com/wpa/tr/pap/intro.htm, accessed February 2006.

2. Charles E. Schaeffer, "Play Therapy for Adults," Psychceu.com, October 2002, http://www.psychceu.com/Schaefer/adults.asp.

3. Williamson, "Introduction," In *Playful Activities.*

4. William Glasser Institute, "Choice Theory," http://www.wglasser.com/index.php?option=com_content&task=view&id=12&Itemid=27, accessed August 14, 2008.

5. D. W. Winnicott, "Playing: Its Theoretical Status in the Clinical Situation." *Int. J. Psychoanal* 49:591–99 (1968).

6. Hara Estroff Marano, "The Power of Play," *Psychology Today*, July/August 1999, http://cms.psychologytoday.com/articles/pto-19990701-000030.html.

7. Williamson, "Introduction," In *Playful Activities.*

8. Marano, "The Power of Play."

9. See particularly the works of Lloyd P. Rieber, Lola Smith, and David Noah. "The Value of Serious Play," *Educational Technology* 38:6, http://it.coe.uga.edu/~lrieber/valueofplay.html; and Lloyd P. Rieber, "Seriously Considering Play: Designing Interactive Learning Environments Based on the Blending of Microworlds, Simulations, and Games" *Educational Technology Research & Development* 44:2, http://it.coe.uga.edu/~lrieber/play.html.

10. Williamson, "Introduction," In *Playful Activities.*

11. Marano, "The Power of Play."

12. Rieber, "Seriously Considering Play."

13. Marano, "The Power of Play."

14. "Shore Leave," *Star Trek, the original series*, DVD, wri. Theodor Sturgeon, (Hollywood: Paramount, 1966). A thank you is due to my trusted former assistant, Jennifer MacCashland, who brought this playful quote to my attention.

15. Marano, "The Power of Play."

16. Brian Sutton-Smith, "Cultivating Courage through Play," *Voices: The New York Journal of Folk Lore* 30 (Spring/Summer 2004), http://www.nyfolklore.org/pubs/voic30-1-2/courage.html.

17. Marano, "The Power of Play."

18. Cross Creek Family Counseling, "What Is Play Therapy?" http://www.crosscreekcounseling.com/play_therapy.html.

19. Williamson, "Introduction," In *Playful Activities*.

20. Pat Kane, "Play For Today," *The Guardian Observer*, October 22, 2000, http://observer.guardian.co.uk/life/story/0,6903,386013,00.html.

21. Matthew 18:3.

22. Marano, "The Power of Play."

23. Some will argue, and rightfully so, that loving God is *as important* as loving others.

24. Be cautious about walking with large puppets in the children's wing or when children are present in the sanctuary because they sometimes frighten younger children.

25. Spencer Johnson, *Who Moved My Cheese?: An Amazing Way to Deal with Change in Your Work and in Your Life* (New York: Putnam, 1998).

26. James Harnish, *You Only Have to Die: Leading Your Congregation to New Life* (Nashville: Abingdon Press, 2004), 56.

8

Be a Hospital for Sinners, Not a Hotel for Saints

One of the saddest memories in my ministry comes from when I was serving as an associate regional minister. I had been asked by the pastor of a particular (though not peculiar) congregation to preach at their morning worship service and arrived at the church with a colleague about ninety minutes before the service was scheduled to begin.

As we had anticipated, the pastor was teaching a Sunday school class and was not available to meet us, so my friend and I went into the sanctuary to wait; there we found several adults already sitting throughout the room (though none were sitting together). Over the course of the next few minutes, each of them would glance our way several times; but none of them would speak or allow us to make eye contact until I began to pass through the sanctuary and greet them with a "good morning" (something that does not come naturally or easily to me).

As I was greeting them, I could not help but wonder whether they were guests in need of meeting or members (and, if so, why they were in the sanctuary rather than in the Sunday school). About forty-five minutes after our arrival, a retired minister who now attended that church came in, spoke to each of the folks in the pews, and came to the front of the sanctuary to warmly greet us. After learning who we were, he asked if we had any needs and then introduced us to another minister's family who had since entered the sanctuary. Soon after that, the congregation's pastor arrived and we moved toward worship.

STANDING ALONE

At the end of the service, the pastor invited everyone to go to the fellowship hall for some "fellowship." The midsize fellowship hall was filled with groups of people; many were standing in a long refreshment line and others were clustered in groups of three and four. As my colleague and I made our way through the line (an endeavor that took nearly fifteen minutes), the only people who spoke to us were those to whom we spoke first. You might say it felt more like a refreshment room than a fellowship hall.

While we were waiting, I also noticed that the retired pastor who had so warmly greeted us earlier was standing by himself in the middle of the room with his coffee and cookie in hand. After getting a cup of punch myself, I tried to maneuver around the room (as denominational folks are generally wont to do), looking for opportunities to either join or strike up a conversation. I succeeded in some small chit-chat for a moment here and there, but, in all honesty, I think I spent more time panning the room looking for the next possibility than I did in substantial conversation. And each time I glanced around, I could not help but notice the retired pastor standing alone in the middle of the room.

It was not as though the retired pastor was trying to be unfriendly; indeed, I could identify with his attempts. Over the course of twenty-five or so minutes, I wondered who might be open to his efforts to speak with them, but no one took his bait. He, too, spent more time on his own than in the random triviality of exchanging a sentence or two. As my colleague and I prepared to leave, I noticed once again that the retired pastor was still standing alone. After sharing in a delightful final few moments with him before we left, I watched him set down his cup, roll up his shirtsleeves, and begin to clean up around the room.

In retrospect, I am glad I stopped on my way out that day and had the opportunity to speak to that retired pastor one last time: the following week we received word that he had passed away. With the news of his passing came the sad realization that that warm pastor had spent his last

Sunday in a Christian community—a community he had loved and faithfully served for decades—standing alone in the middle of a hall set aside for *fellowship*. Imagine if he had been a stranger there.

A lot of our churches are more closed than open. In deference to the efforts of that retired pastor, many of us act as though we are hotels for the saints rather than hospitals for the sinners. We have already spoken about our tendencies to want to be served rather than to serve. Neither are we always the warmest, friendliest, or most welcoming lot. And even when we are, often the friendliness is only skin deep. We want people in our pews or classrooms, but not in our lives.

HOSPITALITY

What we are talking about here is hospitality, the act of warmly and generously making people feel welcome. Welcome and acceptance are indispensable for churches that want to reach those without a church home. Except for the influence of the pastor, welcome and acceptance are key reasons cited by new church members for why they return to a church; and they are the most common reasons given for why folks join a particular congregation. And the fear of not being accepted is often cited as the number one barrier to visiting a church.

We all have our repertoire of good and bad stories of church hospitality. Since we are talking about time bombs here, let me offer some of the bad: like the stories of folks being asked to move to another row because they were "sitting in someone else's seat."

Or the woman who for six months attended a church of 150 participants (not a large church by any means) when a key leader literally bumped into her in the hallway and said, "Oh, you're so-and-so." The woman had passed the leader many times around the church, but he had never given her enough opportunity for even the briefest of verbal exchanges. The guest was curious about how this person might know her name, so she asked him and he said that he had asked the pastor some time before. She wondered why he had never bothered to come and ask her. . . .

Or the time my family (Bill, myself, and all five of our then teenage children) visited a small church in a suburban setting. During the morning greeting time all guests were asked to stand, and the compliant

Tenny-Brittians did. I am not sure who was more embarrassed: the seven guests or the congregation as they mumbled some song about "how happy we are to see you." For all their "happiness," no one but the pastor spoke to us after the service.

Then there are the churches where people literally turn their backs on those who "don't look like us," and walk away from hands extended for shaking. Or the ushers who bark, "Take off that hat" to the guests' children who have come proudly wearing their Little League caps.

Yet hospitality is more than a mere "hello" or "peace be with you," more than coffee and goodies before or after the service. To be sure, those are important; but they are only vehicles for extending hospitality; they help to create an environment where hospitality can be expressed and experienced.

Hotel Hospitality

For a short time during seminary I had the opportunity to work for one of the Ritz-Carlton hotels in Atlanta, Georgia. Perhaps you have heard of the Ritz-Carlton chain: it is known for its luxury and commitment to excellence. The folks at the Ritz-Carlton—from management to banqueting to housekeeping to the front desk to part-time word processors working at night—know the importance of providing an environment of "genuine care and comfort."[2] But more than that, they know that creating a place that is caring and comforting can provide an experience that "enlivens the senses, instills well-being, and fulfills even the unexpressed wishes and needs of their guests."[3]

Now, before you say that we have suddenly switched from talking about churches to talking about luxury hotels, let me say that there are a number of churches that strive to be places of genuine care and comfort in the vein of the Ritz-Carlton. While not always the most luxurious of places, these churches strive to enliven the senses of participants and to inspire and instill well-being so that folks can be better prepared and able to invite and welcome others into their fold. And while places of caring and comfort, these churches are more like hospitals than hotels; they do not stop at opening the doors and welcoming guests with a smile upon their arrival and departure.

106

Hospital Hospitality

Churches committed to hospital hospitality are mobilized to do "triage" on those who come to them, to help folks assess their spiritual needs and offer "prescriptions" to address them. The more holistic churches are set to assess and address social, emotional, mental, and even physical needs. They also resemble hospitals more than hotels because the guests are not there to be pampered (welcomed and well-taken care of, yes); they are there to get healthy, or healthier, so they can live the lives God has given them to live. Indeed, Dictionary.com offers that the act of being hospitable is favorable to growth and development.[4]

Messy Hospitality

I realize that your church may not be the most hospitable, but let me step back for a moment and say that for many years I have been saying that hospitality is not one of my gifts. I love to sit with people and talk or play, but I dislike the preparations enough that entertaining can be a chore if I let it (I was raised with an understanding that "entertaining" demands a clean and orderly house with all the right accoutrements for entertaining). Fortunately, my husband cares much less than do I about the clean house part and has both the gifts of generosity and hospitality. When you come to our house when both of us are home, you will more than likely find the house orderly; but, more important, we (or Bill) will feed you well and otherwise take care of you.

When Bill is not here, you may find conversation but little else. My friends know well that you can visit me for five or six hours and never get more than a simple glass of water or cup of tea unless you ask for it. I used to beat myself up about that, but not too long ago I realized that while I do not have the gift of hospitality, I am no less a hospitable person in my own right, having cultivated an ability to provide an environment for holding care and extending comfort.

I have learned that hospitality is really much more about *who* than *what* I offer. When friends and strangers come to our home, they know (or soon learn) they can find a listening ear, a shoulder to cry on, a word or two of encouragement, and a prayer. In reality, hospitality is not necessarily some*thing* we offer but, rather, is the offering of ourselves . . . and with ourselves, the tangible touch of Jesus.

Your congregation may be more like me in that it does not easily set a nice spread, or it may be like a few churches I have known and loved who did better to not offer refreshments because of their dangerously overt disrespect of hospitality. The real question is, though, "How are you offering the tangible touch of Jesus?"

Hear this: the question is not, "Are you offering "teaching *about* Jesus?" or "worship *for* Jesus?" but, rather, "How are you offering *the tangible touch of* Jesus." How are you being Jesus for those who come to and through your doors? The first level of hospitality is to make people feel warm, welcome, and accepted; but the next level—offering that tangible touch—is all the more important for them . . . and for surviving the transformational journey.

Hospitality Begins at Home

Indeed, hospitality is another one of those key environments for holding transformation. And for this reason it is all the more important to ensure that hospitality has begun, and is established, at home—among ourselves—before we try to extend it to those in our midst. Many churches are full of members who do not like one another; yet many of these churches eagerly want to bring new folks into this unfortunate mix. Sadly, it is not uncommon to hear long-time church members say how unaccepted or unwelcome they feel in their own congregation. Often we think about hospitality as what we extend to guests or to those we otherwise do not yet know; but it has to start at home. If we have not learned how to tangibly touch those with whom we share a church home, we are not yet ready to reach out and touch someone else.

Several years ago I lost a significant amount of weight, to the extent that it was not uncommon for me to pass unrecognized by friends and close colleagues. In many ways it provided opportunities to rethink how people (myself included) react to, and interact with, one another.

It began to hit home when a clergy colleague seemed to be avoiding me at our clergy meetings. I had worked with this pastor and his church on several occasions, and he had always been cordial and relatively conversational; but all that stopped after I had missed a couple of meetings. For two months after my return, I made a concerted effort to catch his attention or, at the least, to wave "hi" or "good-bye," but I could not get anywhere near him. After experiencing his glancing in my direction and turning his back on me a couple of different times, I began to wonder if he had something going on his life or, just as troubling, that I might have done something to offend him. Later I tried to ask him, but he was always engaged in deep conversation with others. I never was able to get close enough to follow up, and I will confess that neither time nor motivation allowed me to pursue figuring out what might be going on.

Several months later we were both in another city for a conference and I passed him on the street and smiled as I greeted him. He replied with the muffled "hi" you would extend to any stranger you walk past, and then I heard him say to his walking partner, "I think that's Kris Tenny-Brittian! I didn't recognize her." I turned around and saw them turned around and went to exchange a few "how-are-you's?" It hit me then that he had not been avoiding me, only looking past me. When I saw him at the next month's meeting, he was back to his cordial and friendly self.

When we are in public, it is easy to look past those we do not recognize and know. In some ways this is a coping mechanism that helps us filter out a potential overload of information; as such, we tend to hone in on those we recognize rather than on those we do not. It is part of the reason why long-time members can complain "no one is coming to church" when the number of new faces in a transforming congregation exceed those who have been there for twenty or so years. What those long-timers are saying in essence is, "I recognize fewer people . . . and do not recognize far too many."

And it is interesting to see who recognizes whom, as some people are more "recognizable" in some congregations than in others. I know of one congregation that instantly sees "single" women who are around thirty years of age and couples in their seventies. If you show up to that church with children, you are likely to pass through those doors virtually unnoticed by anyone other than the pastor and the couple of others who have children themselves. Single women in their fifties can slide in and out with no other greeting than from the pastor and whoever hands them a bulletin. But be a young woman attending by yourself or a couple in your seventies and you can guarantee that at least four people have contacted the pastor to make sure he knows you have been there. Another church I know has their radar set for married couples with children. If you are a single parent or a couple without children in tow, you will likely slip through their proverbial cracks.

These slips go beyond mission, vision, and targeted demographics; they are about our ability, and inability, to see certain people. Sometimes I wonder how—or why—the "ignored" populations ever join the churches into which they slide virtually unseen and unknown, where few know their names. And, amazingly, these folks are often faithful, loyal members who give of their time and talent year in and year out.

Beyond the dismal fact that some of us actively dislike one another and others of us are unconscious of those with whom we worship, one of the challenges many of us face is that we have not been conditioned to translate our at-home hospitality into the church or related settings. Perhaps it is because we, ourselves, feel more like strange guests than hosts or active participants there. But think for a moment about those you might entertain in your home. Some people are known to say, "The first time you come to my house you're a guest; after that, you're on your own." While each translates that statement in a slightly different way, in general it means, "You are always welcome here. . . . Now, help yourself." Nonetheless, each time I pass through their doors, I am warmly and personally greeted by name and with a hug. And if they are too busy to chit-chat when I arrive, they will make time to follow up before I leave.

Radical Hospitality

Now, we have to figure out how to translate that kind of hospitality into our churches. We have to figure out how to see the folks who come through our doors—friends and strangers alike. We have to greet one another personally and maybe even with a hug, even when we're too busy to talk. We have to figure out ways to focus on people's needs each week, and through the week, so we can care for and help one another be comfortable but not so comfortable that we slip into the hotel, or

Prince's Cruise Lines, mentality and forget that we are first and foremost a hospital.

To be sure, the church is called to an even greater level of hospitality than we can experience in the finest of hotels, that level known as *radical hospitality*. Jesus' words about the separation of sheep and goats comes to mind when talking about radical hospitality:

> Then the king will say to those at his right hand, "Come, you that are blessed by my Father, inherit the kingdom prepared for you from the foundation of the world; for I was hungry and you gave me food, I was thirsty and you gave me something to drink, I was a stranger and you welcomed me, I was naked and you gave me clothing, I was sick and you took care of me, I was in prison and you visited me.[5]

This level of hospitality is challenging and is not for the congregation who is not yet successfully practicing hospitality among their own ranks.

In fact, radical hospitality can actually be detrimental to a church. If you do not believe me, start openly inviting and welcoming people who have been traditionally marginalized in your congregation (whomever those may be for you: homeless, homosexuals, transsexuals, heterosexuals, Hispanics, Caucasians, whomever). One congregation I pastored claimed to be radically hospitable, but that did not preclude the board from having extensive conversations about why transgendered women should not be allowed to use the women's bathroom. While our practice of radical hospitality was hailed by some, it—and we—was publicly denounced by others. Some weeks we found ourselves spending more time speaking on behalf of radical hospitality than desiring to practice it.

EXTENDING HOSPITALITY INTO THE WIDE, OPEN SPACES

Hospitality extends beyond invitation and welcome; it commands us to seriously practice the arts of care and comfort. I am reminded of a congregation with three long-time members who suffered from mental illnesses that had at various times over the decades manifested in public "scenes." Most of the other long-timers took one of two approaches to the three: (1) avoid them or (2) parent them. All of the "special needs" adults were extremely bright people with amazing talents, yet for decades they had been in that church with little or no opportunities to share themselves wholly with their brothers and sisters. Then a pastor joined the staff who brought with her a value of hospitality and the perception that everyone has something to bring and add to worship. She befriended these folks and got to know their passions and talents . . . but not in some paternalistic, patronizing manner.

Within a year after that pastor's arrival, one of the "crazy members,"[6] who had been a member of that congregation for forty years, was for the first time contributing and sharing her remarkable gifts of cooking, writing, prayer, and faith—not only in that congregation but with others beyond. And what's more, she also began to experience a new level of wholeness with her birth family and children.

Coincidence? No, this is one of many examples of the level of healing and wholeness that can occur in the people with whom we minister when we allow ourselves to radically move into true hospitality. But it requires finding ways to be open to, listening for, and recognizing folks in our midst, whether or not they belong to "us."

If your congregation is having trouble with this step, appoint two to four people each Sunday to "scope out" those they do not recognize. Then all they have to do is go by, extend their hands, and offer their names and a "hello" and "glad you are here." Of course, it helps if you can get their names and addresses or phone numbers for follow-up, but that is another book. If you're courageous, sit with them.

Don't worry that they may say to you, "I have been a member here for twenty-two years"; bite your tongue and do *not* tell them that it is interesting you have not seen them in the two years you have been there. Instead, reiterate how glad you are to make their acquaintance and make an appointment to get to know them better over coffee or lunch (and be sure to keep the appointment). It is not enough to merely invite—or expect—folks to come; we have to receive them, integrate them into our lives, and allow ourselves to be integrated into theirs.

Being a hospital for sinners connotes a willingness to be more than a place folks come to check out and hopefully check into. For all their supposed saintliness, hotels can be fraught with the time bombs of insincerity, unwelcome, unacceptance, and disillusionment. Hospitals look for the open spaces where people are standing alone, whether that's in the sanctuary or a refreshment room, whether at a meeting or at midnight. And we have to do more than just look for them; we have to speak to them and invite them into our lives.

Notes

1. Jaqueline E. Wenger with Martha Grace Reese and J. Kristina Tenny-Brittian, "Summary of Responses for 'Survey of Evangelism in Mainline Churches,' A Study of Mainline Churches Performing High Numbers of Adult Baptisms," http://gracenet.info/documents/Wenger%20Reese%20Survey%20Report.pdf.

2. *The Ritz-Carlton Hotel*, "The Ritz-Carlton Credo," http://www.ritzcarlton.com/corporate/about_us/gold_standards.asp.

3. Ibid.

4. Dictionary.com, http://dictionary.reference.com/search?.

5. Matthew 25:34–36.

6. This member will tell you that her peers used to think of her as "Crazy Jane."

9

PRACTICE THE
FINE ART OF
CONVERSATION

A few friends and I once gathered underneath a bridge with others from around the Puget Sound area to help provide dinner to more than a hundred homeless men, women, and children. Actually, it was the second gathering for some of us and since our first experience, the ad hoc organizers had moved the start time back an hour (a little detail we had missed). Arriving much earlier than necessary, my friend Jennifer and I were met by nervous planners who told us we would have to leave the area and wait somewhere else until the "vendors" were allowed under the bridge to help with the set-up. As we were moving our car, I could not help but notice the homeless folks who had started gathering early for dinner. Like us, they were prevented from accessing the lot underneath the bridge, so they had begun to line up along the outside of a fence that separated the lot from some old buildings.

As the hour appointed for set-up approached, Jennifer and I moved our car back beneath the bridge and met up with my daughter Katrina and scores of other "vendors" who were now descending upon the lot. It was a rush of activity to get everything ready for the dinner: a huge barbeque was fired up, tables were being set in place, yellow rope lines were being established, and people were scurrying around trying to figure out where to best position the food they had brought to share. We, too, were trying to figure out where to put the fruit we had brought, but I could not help but notice the growing gathering of homeless folks on the other side of the fence.

While this was an incredible mission, I have to admit I still have mixed feelings about that scene. On the one hand, I am moved by the hospitality that, regardless of the weather, unofficially brings out those scores of folks to feed those with no house of their own . . . those who extend a hospitality that attempts to communicate care and concern. But I cannot get the fence out of my mind and the way the "vendors" (as though we were selling that hospitality) gather on one side and the "homeless" gather on the other, with our point of contact coming as "they" stand on one side of the tables—within the yellow rope line, please—and "we" stand on the other. And although those tables are only about eighteen inches wide, they might as well be a canyon when it comes to extending the authentic hospitality about which we were just speaking.

I am well aware of the need for safety and the reality that a lot of us would probably not venture out beneath a bridge to rub shoulders with folks who live differently than we do, some (though, by no means, all) of whom suffer from serious mental illness. In reality, a number of the vendors would probably be much more reticent to come—if they would come at all—without the lines, tables, and fence. But, sadly, our reticence often translates into reluctance to do little more than provide well-intentioned, much-needed handouts to others . . . in essence, to communicate care and concern through actions with as few words as possible attached.

I do not want to demean or denigrate the vital feeding and assistance programs going on around the country and the world. But two more thoughts come to mind. First, we Christians often provide a piece of bread without offering the Bread of Life (that is, without offering the good news of a relationship with Jesus Christ himself). Many of us have heard the old saying, "Give a person a fish and you feed that person for a day; teach a person to fish and feed that person for life." But think about this variation for a moment: "Build a [person] a fire and [that person]'s warm for a day. Set a [person] on fire and [that person]'s warm for the rest of his [or her] life!"

Indeed, people need food but they also need relationships and opportunities to belong: with others and with the One who can set their lives on fire.

Like you and me, most homeless people want to be valued for the people they are beneath the outward fact of having no house. Homeless folks are more in need of hand-ups than hand-outs, and that very fact comes back to a level of hospitality that moves past motions and evolves into establishing relationships that will allow "us" to get to know "them" as individuals. And, beyond the personal relationships, we have a mandate—a Great Commandment—to introduce others to, and help them develop their relationships with, Jesus Christ.

The other thought that pierces my heart as I replay that scene under the bridge is that it starkly mirrors what we see happening in churches around the country. Although I haven't yet been in a church with yellow rope lines, I have been in far too many where the conversations over potluck dinners never move much past "Hello" and "How are you?" Week in and week out I hear yet more examples of the invisible fences that separate groups of folks into the cliques for which too many churches are notorious. Parishioners are separated from pastors. Pastors are separated from their parishioners. Parishioners separate themselves from one another. And then there is the separation of those in the pews from the people who cautiously venture inside our proverbial doors.

One of the classes I have found myself teaching on a number of occasions is "Introductions 101" that covers the basics of how to introduce one's self and others to the new people in our midst. Indeed, in churches introductions and quality conversation seem to be lost or forgotten arts.

THE LOST ART OF CONVERSATION

A couple of years ago I had the opportunity to spend a long lunch at the home of a young mother and her preschooler. It was a delightful, no-stress time of sharing and getting to know one another better that made me leave there missing the extended time my once young children and I used to spend nearly every day with the special people in our lives.

I think fondly about those days when I juggled work, school, and nearly single parenting and had to walk or take the bus everywhere because we did not have a car; but each afternoon we seemed to find the time to spend an hour or two sitting on porches or in the kitchen, chatting with neighbors about our days and whatever else might come to mind. I remember, too, how conversations such as those turned into things like vacation Bible schools beyond our wildest imaginations and, once, into an effort with other young mothers to successfully seek significant changes in the elementary school our children attended.

And I cannot help but wonder how my days got so full—and with what—so that I now seem to have time only for quick e-mail exchanges, brief conversations with my husband and at-home children over dinner (on those rare occasions when we get to have dinner together), a phone call to a daughter once a week or so, and only a couple of longer phone calls with a couple of long-distance friends every couple of weeks if I'm lucky. Many days I long for those "lazier" afternoons, or at least for the depth of conversation and relationships they afforded; and I wonder how I might reprioritize my life to accommodate it.

How about you? How much time are you spending in real conversation and relationship-building with the people around you? But, wait. . . . Before you jump to answer that question, take into account Rabbi Noah Weinberg's reminder that there is a difference between conversation and discussion:

> A "discussion" is an issue of right or wrong, a cerebral exchange of facts and opinions. A "conversation" is a personal exploration of another person. The point of conversation is not to impress others or to enhance your popularity, but to learn about others. That is our most common mistake.[2]

Indeed, speaking is something most of us do naturally; however, true conversation is an art.

Loren Ekroth, an expert on business and social conversation, observes that true conversation is more than a tool for transmitting information. He notes that conversation is "also a means of building families and communities, enhancing learning, healing emotions, mediating disputes, and solving complex international problems.[3] And while many of us already engage in conversation for these reasons, too few of us do so with these intentions in mind. In other words, too many of us are taking conversation for granted.[4]

Perhaps you are familiar with the recommendation that people ("we") need to get up out of our office chairs and walk down the hallways to talk to an associate rather than e-mailing him or her. It makes me think how many times I used to e-mail my assistant whose office was separated from mine by a thin wall. Rather than walk out of my office door, take ten steps to the right, and walk into her office; I would shoot her an e-mail. After all, why waste the time to get up, let alone invite verbal communication? Even when we lived in a house with less than 1800 square feet, my husband and I would sit in our respective home offices and toss e-mails back and forth about dinner or lunch plans. Today we Skype or use our Blackberry Messenger between our home offices rather than pick up the intercom or walk up or down the stairs. Why waste the time? Or is time spent in human touch a waste? While e-mail and instant messages can be innocuous, we often forget that these are correspondence, not conversation.

Think for a moment about the ways in which e-mail, text messaging, instant messaging, and Skype have replaced conversation. How many times have you found yourself "conversing" via e-mail rather than by phone or in person? Each month brings new alternatives for communication brevity. In fact, via e-mail and instant messaging, we can

LOL (laugh out loud);

:-) (smile); and

:-((frown)

as we express our IMHO (in my humble opinion), FWIW (for what it's worth), and so on. But we miss something when we miss out on the opportunity to hear those laughs and see those smiles and frowns for ourselves. Today, some twelve-step groups that recommend a certain number of outreach calls per day are wrestling with whether or not e-mail outreach has the same effect as voice-to-voice contact. My son, Britt, has noticed that people will say, "L-O-L" rather than actually laugh out loud in response to something funny; they seem to be mentally responding rather than physically and emotionally responding.

Another problem with the move to electronic communication is that we have no body language to read. Without body language (or the voice inflections and modulations telephone conversations afford) each reader gets to place emphasis and, as a result, interpretation where she or he deems appropriate . . . often not where intended by the writer. This can lead to confusion and mixed messages that add another layer of "stuff" to the already murky transformational journey.

The church would do well ourselves to think a bit more about all this, particularly as more of us are adopting clauses into our governing documents that allow for e-mail voting. Although apparently efficient, e-mail voting can efface a level of discernment and wisdom that comes only with interpersonal interaction . . . with conversation. Brevity is not always better.

Talking "about," Speaking "to," and Conversing "with"

Thinking about e-mail reminds us that conversation is an exchange between two or more people. Loren Ekroth puts it this way: "Conversation is not a solo act. Usually it is a duet. Sometimes it's a trio or quartet, and occasionally it's a group sing-a-long.["5]

You will notice that, as Rabbi Weinberg cautioned us earlier, conversation is more than one-sided, or otherwise disjointed, communication. It involves give and take, mutual exchange (although that exchange may not always be harmonious). We call this "conversing *with*" people.

In contrast to conversing with people, many of us are guilty of talking *about* people or situations. Something or someone drives us up the wall and we will talk about it to everyone else but the person who can actually do something directly about it: the "culprit" him- or herself. And even when we do muster up the nerve or whatever it takes to speak to someone, that is often exactly how our conversation proceeds: we speak *to*, rather than converse *with*, them. We often fall far short of entering into two-way conversation. Loren Ekroth notes that "some people behave as if conversation is a monologue with an audience rather than . . . a collaboration, a verbal dance.["6] My friend Carol Macaulay will ask people, "Are you talking for the sake of speaking, or do you want people to hear you?" There is a difference between talking to folks and conversing with them.

As far as talking *about* folks, the Bible has a few things to say about that. In the book of Leviticus we are told not to go about "as a slanderer among your people."[7] The sixteenth chapter of Proverbs reminds us that a "perverse person spreads strife, and a whisperer separates close friends."[8] The New International Version of the Bible translates that word "whisperer" as "gossip." Often, we polite folk in the church are reticent to use that word" "gossip" for talking about others; but that is exactly what it is: "rumor or talk of a personal, sensational, or intimate nature."[9] In his letter to the Romans, Paul lists gossips and slanderers with the "God-haters, insolent, haughty, boastful, inventors of evil."[10] And the Greek word for devil, *diabolos*, is also the word used for those given to malicious gossip.[11]

There is a reason why gossips are called demons. Words have a lot of power. We know that we humans can talk ourselves into things by the very nature of our words. Tell me you "can't" do something, and I am most certain you never will. But our words hurt more than ourselves. I cringed the night I dodged a little girl in a restaurant and her mother grabbed her arm saying, "Get out of the lady's way, Stupid." I did not feel much like a lady that night as my heart went out to that little girl and I wanted to speak harsher words to her mother.

I have learned not to take lightly the scripture that tells us that "whatever [we] bind on earth will be bound in heaven, and whatever [we] loose on earth will be loosed in heaven."[12] One interpretation of that passage holds that what we speak will be. If you tell me, "Your plan will never work," in a sense you are cursing it so it will never work. When we tell ourselves we are failures, we bind ourselves to failing. When we tell someone they are stupid, they may likely be—or become—stupid. Conversely, when we speak the best into people or situations or ourselves, we release the possibilities that are within.

On a more positive note, we also have scriptures that inform transformational dialogue. One of the most foundational is Matthew 18:15–18. Here Jesus tells us:

> If another member of the church sins against you, go and point out the fault when the two of you are alone. If the member listens to you, you have regained that one. But if you are not listened to, take one or two others along with you, so that every

word may be confirmed by the evidence of two or three witnesses. If the member refuses to listen to them, tell it to the church; and if the member refuses to listen even to the church, let such a one be to you as a Gentile and a tax-collector.

Teaching and living this directive is not easy. I have long been an advocate of speaking the truth in love and try to be as honest as possible in ways that people can hear me. Sometimes this means waiting longer than I, or others, might like to have a conversation with someone else because people are not always able to hear when we are ready to speak.

I rarely approach potentially difficult discussions without divine guidance and prayers for God's intervention. I regularly ask God to filter what comes out of my mouth so that God's words are heard rather than my own. For conversations *with* people, it is important to know what might get in the way of another person's being able to hear what we are trying to think: words that might set them off, situations or examples that might skew their thinking or hearing.

LEARNING TO CONVERSE "WITH"

Being able to speak the truth in love so we are heard also generally dictates being in a relationship with those with whom we speak. In Greek, the words of Matthew 18:15 that we translated above as "another member of the church" actually come from two words, αδελφος σου: *adelphos sou*: your brother. The very nature of Matthew's "your brother" (or sister) connotes there is a relationship. We are meant to be in such a relationship with others that we can have real and authentic conversations with them, so that we can express our feelings and concerns without concern that we will be shut down or devalued. First and foremost, we are meant to be in relationship with people (just as we are meant to be in relationship with God). The goal is to develop relationships with people that are authentic and conducive to cultivating depth, transparency, and honesty.

Such relationships tend not to come easily (particularly in congregations experiencing transformation); and we need to be cautious, practicing Jesus' advice about being as shrewd as snakes while being as innocent as doves.[13] We leaders, too, need to extend our training and experiences to the practice of true dialogue. That means putting a stop to our own bent toward talking about others rather than speaking to or conversing with them. That means practicing and become adept at stopping people in mid-harangue and pointing them in the direction of the person about whom they are complaining.

It is difficult, but it can be done. I learned—though I am far from perfect—the importance of this principle during one of my pastorates. It started as a "duh" when a part-time staff member was unhappy about a full-time staff hire, a pastor whom the staff member himself had first introduced and recommended. Soon after the hire, the staff member was in my office with her "concerns" about the new pastor, concerns that were actually more about the staff member than the pastor; I suggested she talk directly to the new pastor about her concerns.

Things seemed to get better, but then the new pastor was soon expressing his concerns about the staff member. We decided to work together in staff meetings to model healthy ways of communicating, modeling for each of us the art of conversation and the need to express our concerns to one another, moving into relationships that might allow us to converse *with* one another. One of the learnings from that experience was the need to take—and to give permission for—time-outs during tough conversations, particularly when the conversations moved from conversing with to speaking to. People need to have permission to say, "I cannot hear you right now, I need to take [so many minutes] out." Whether in meetings or in my own household, we always respect that request and break for the requested amount of time.

The staff member who was unhappy about the new pastor eventually left the staff. Interestingly (though not surprisingly), the staff member's replacement seemed to cause another round of "concerns" among staff and the precedent for "talking about" resurfaced. Fortunately, we were able to recognize the patterns and spent many more long hours in staff meetings and in one-on-ones and two-on-twos working on ways everyone could communicate, converse, and work effectively with one another. It became common to walk down the hall in the late afternoon and find staff members with their heads together working through a disagreement . . . getting to know and appreciate and love one another better. And their modeling trickled out into the transforming congregation as they initiated one-on-ones with those whom they knew they needed to establish a better working relationship.

The journey to conversing with folks is not easy, nor is it popular. I took a lot of flack about my leadership style in that congregation: (1) for the commitment to build up my staff rather than replace them, and (2) for the amount of time I dedicated to nurturing them, particularly from management types who regularly recommended firing one or more of them. On the practical side, there was not enough time or money to replace these staff people some might have considered "in development" (or not ready to be on staff).

On this side of the experience, though, a healthy, effective staff emerged that was capable of relational transparency, ever-growing spiritual depth, and the ability to do difficult ministry in an unhealthy ministry setting. In addition, I learned the privilege of staff development and the joy that comes with it. Several years later, I remain in contact with each of those pastors and their families, and they all stay in contact with one another—even though we all now live and minister across the country from one another. Each one of them now also serves in a significant leadership capacity.

Moving from talking about, to speaking to, to conversing with people is not only a staff issue, though. It is about developing healthy, holy communication and the practices that support it. The rise of conversation cafes suggests that conversation is a lost art, one that is wont to be reclaimed. Kenneth Haugk's *Speaking the Truth in Love* reminds us that "individuals are response-able,"[14] we are capable of responding . . . of conversing. Imagine what might happen if we learned to actually converse in our conversations and move it into our families, our friendship networks, our neighborhoods, our places of employment, our local businesses, and our governments. Might we defuse a time bomb or two? We might even see a change in the way conversation is engaged and problems are resolved in the world! What a difference our preparation for conversation would make, especially as we developed and demonstrated it in the toughest of situations.

The need to converse with, rather than talk about or merely speak to, people is particularly significant for holding the transformational journey that I list it in this next-to-the-final chapter: it is *not* to be forgotten! The journey of transformation is difficult enough with those we do not like or care to talk to; the difficulties compound exponentially when we are unable to engage our companions—our brothers and sisters—in the conversations that are necessary for mutual growth and solution-finding. How can we develop skills and find ways to move from talking about to conversing with the people in our churches? How can we in positions of leadership model, teach, and reiterate those skills for those with whom, and to whom, we minister?

CONVERSATIONAL TIPS

There are, of course, some basics for creating environments that can hold artful conversation. Loren Ekroth frames conversation as, ideally, a cooperative process, even when one of the parties does not want to cooperate (such as when a parent tries to converse with his sulking, sullen teen, or a counselor speaks to a reticent client). Though it is not always easy, we can often move past one-sided communication by inviting cooperation.[15]

The art of conversation has a lot to do with *how* we converse. It is important to strive for mutuality and respect. Please note that although a number of churches have a value of *tolerance*, we are talking about *respect* here. Tolerance dictates that we "put up" with what someone else says; respect encourages us to try to understand what others are trying to say, even when we disagree with what we are hearing.

Indeed, it is not necessary for us to agree with what someone else is saying. Here, though, we are challenged to refrain from becoming (or sounding) argumentative and to try to walk away from our conversations with at least mutual understanding. Mortimer Adler offers that the first rule of good conversation is to neither agree nor disagree until we understand the other person's position.[16] In reality, we are unable to agree or disagree until both parties come to understand a particular question or issue in the same way; to do otherwise is to find ourselves speaking past one another.

This speaking past one another is commonly found in transformational settings, often during exchanges about lack of congregational growth. Two people—or even opposing "sides"—think they are speaking to the concern of congregational growth when one may be talking about the lack of new people coming in through the front doors and the other is talking about the exodus of long-timers through the back door. Yes, they are both talking about a lack of growth, but one is concerned with the long-timers and the other with a lack of evangelism. Conversational mutuality dictates that both "sides" hear one another and then, together in turn, address each other's concerns. Once we identify and understand our concerns, we can establish a basis for talking about the lack of growth.

Conversation _with_ takes a lot of time, energy, and commitment. It is easier for most of us to walk away from a disagreement than to see it through to agreement. In fact, many of us have doubts about whether many disagreements can actually ever move into agreement. However, Mortimer Adler offers four statements that can allow us to verbalize the grounds of a disagreement and urge it toward mutual understanding and resolution:

1. "I think you hold that position because you are unaware of facts or reasons that will have a critical bearing on it." When using this statement, be prepared to offer the missing information you think will have a bearing on his or her point of view.

2. "I think you hold that position because you have been misinformed about matters that are critically relevant." Again, be prepared to indicate the misinformation the other person has been given, as well as the correct information that will lead that person to alter his or her position.

3. "You seem to be well informed and have a firm grasp of the evidence and reasons that support your position, but I think you have drawn the wrong conclusions because of a mistake in reasoning." Then be ready to gently point out the logical errors that, if corrected, would lead to a different conclusion.

4. "You have obviously done some homework and have logically come to this conclusion, but I think that your thinking about the subject is incomplete. If we think this through a bit further, we can reach other conclusions that somewhat alter or qualify the one you have

reached." Make sure you are able to point out alternative conclusions and how they can alter the position taken by the other person.[17]

Statements such as Adler's allow us to further explore our own positions and suppositions. Authentic communication depends on our ability to admit when we are talking from our feelings rather than from "the facts" as we understand them. Adler's statements can also hold us in check as we seek clarity about our position on a particular question, concern, situation, or problem. In our attempts to help others be accurate in what they say and think, we can better consider our own trains of thought and speak more accurately and effectively, defusing time bombs along the way.

However, defusing time bombs with the fine art of conversation necessitates that we avoid being judgmental, create spaces for people to think and process, and pass up opportunities to escalate diatribes into arguments. When you cannot find or create a space for conversation, agree to walk away when the atmosphere gets critical, confrontational, or is otherwise no longer conducive to conversation.

Mutual and respectful conversation always strives for understanding and demands a resolution.[18] It is never enough to walk away from a disagreement without an appointment to follow up. Neither is it enough to walk away from an agreement or mutual understanding without some kind of follow-up. On the practical side, many a perceived understanding has dissolved over time and distance. On the ideal side, agreements allow us to mobilize and move into appropriate actions.

Conversation is an exchange of thoughts, opinions, information, and feelings; it is not meant to be an egotistical exercise. What we bring to a conversation is our own perspective and version of the truth, neither *the* truth nor the *whole* truth.[19] Thinking otherwise is a sure way to quickly negate the possibility for a conversation of any depth.

Another caveat regarding effective conversation is to be careful about "rehearsing" potential conversations. While there is value in this approach, it can also be detrimental. Conversations are meant to be guided by what we hear. When we focus our attention on what we are planning to say, or on what we will say next, we step out of our listening mode, away from our responsibility to listen to what someone else is saying, and risk responding inappropriately or incongruently. Effective conversation is an intricately woven dynamic of speaking and listening. Loren Ekroth reminds us that merely "taking turns talking does not constitute an effective conversation. It may be an argument, with each speaker rehearsing their points while the other talks. Or it may be two monologues, each in turn. But it's not a conversation."[20] As an exchange, conversation demands that we listen and respond appropriately.

But the art of conversation may be more about why we are conversing than about how we converse. It is helpful to know the purpose of a conversation before delving into it. If, as my friend Carol suggests, we are going to speak so that people will hear what we are saying, we need to know just what it is we are trying to say. Is our purpose for speaking to impart information, support, opinion, or feelings? Often in transformational settings, people who want to communicate their concern end up doing little more than acting out their feelings. It can be frustrating to sit in "fact-finding" meetings and hear little more than opinions and veiled threats.

Knowing what we are wanting to communicate not only helps our conversations become more efficient and less likely to stray or blow up; it helps us with choices like what words to use and when to schedule the conversation, and for where. Do not let yourself get cornered into having a tough conversation in an open or public place. Learn to use phrases such as, "I cannot talk to you about that now, but let us schedule a time when we can have that conversation." By doing so, you are both honoring the person's need to talk to you and nonjudgmentally guiding what would be a "speak to" situation into a potential "conversation with" wherein you may both find some relief, if not a base from which to start working on respect and mutuality.

LEARNING TO CONVERSE

Many of us have either never learned, or have lost, the fine art of conversation. Groups like Toastmasters International and Training Groups ("T-Groups") are good choices for learning how to better converse with, and talk to, others. Conversation Cafés, one of the latest crazes in the

United States, are another good alternative. For those of you who are not lucky enough to have one near you,[21] a Conversation Café is a one and one-half hour facilitated discussion group that is held in a public setting. Each Café session follows a simple format to facilitate opportunities to dialogue with others on a variety of subjects.

Whether or not you ever find yourself at a Conversation Café, the official website offers six "agreements" for a great conversation that we would do well to heed:

1. **Open-mindedness**: listen to and respect all points of view

2. **Acceptance**: suspend judgment as best you can

3. **Curiosity**: seek to understand rather than persuade

4. **Discovery**: question old assumptions, look for new insights

5. **Sincerity**: speak for yourself about what has personal heart and meaning

6. **Brevity**: go for honesty and depth but don't go on and on.[22]

My husband and I informally practice these principles in group gatherings we host in our home. On a regular basis we gather with friends (some in the church, some not yet) to watch a movie or documentary and talk about what we have heard and seen in it. We say that our one rule is that everyone respectfully listen and hold what other people say and think. In addition to lively conversation, we have had the opportunity to get to know others better, as well as ourselves and what we think—and why. Gatherings like these have also proven useful for encouraging conversation, as well as significant relationships. Which brings us back to the fine art of conversation as a holding environment for transformation.

CONVERSING TO SURVIVE THE TRANSFORMATIONAL JOURNEY

The folks at Conversation Café have noted that conversing with others might be "the most radical and healing act we do."[23] It is no secret that people like to talk about, and through, crises. Most of us have sat through multiple recountings of loved ones' surgeries, birth experiences, and/or car accidents. Crises and transformations can be threatening and lead to a need for safety, or at least to feel safe. This need to feel safe can lead us either to open up or shut down.

In congregational transformation we want folks to open up. We know that it is important for folks to connect during times of crisis and that talking about things that disturb us is a helpful tool for processing what we are feeling and thinking. Conversation allows us to both connect and process, and it is all the more important as a holding environment on the transformational journey. We need to know how to authentically and effectively converse if we are going to be able to work out (and not act out) our feelings and our fears. And we have to do more than merely know how to converse; we have to be in good practice to converse if we are going to be able to make the most of discovering and living into solutions—or at least pathways to the next oases—when the opportunities present themselves.

I remember my mother teaching me, "Sticks and stones may break my bones, but names will never harm me." And I remember how many times while growing up I wished that was so. I am grateful to one of my pastors, who told me with great pain, "You know, Kris, it doesn't matter how old you get, it still hurts when they talk behind your back."

Words can bless and they can curse. As curses, they are one of the most dangerous congregational time bombs; and when we expletively explode behind people's backs, we move ever closer to fatal injury. There is no mistake that loving our neighbors as Jesus loves us is as important as loving God. All the transformational efforts in the world will avail nothing if we cannot love God and others as Jesus loves them. We are either blessing or cursing; there really is no middle ground.

At least once a year we hear the words from the thirteenth chapter of the apostle Paul's first letter to the people living in Corinth; but we often apply them only to our loved ones. Read them again here, picturing yourself in conversation with the person you would least like to speak to (let alone converse with):

> Love is patient; love is kind; love is not envious or boastful or
> arrogant or rude. It does not insist on its own way; it is not irri-

table or resentful; it does not rejoice in wrongdoing, but rejoices in the truth. It bears all things, believes all things, hopes all things, endures all things.

Love never ends.[24]

Without figuring out how to converse lovingly and relationally with the brothers and sisters in our congregations, we will never be able to fulfill the Great Commandment and converse with those beyond the church's doors. Forget hospitality . . . playing together . . . staying on course . . . keeping cool, calm, and collected . . . putting the right people in the right places . . . finding the right fit . . . taking only what you need. Forget about facing your money fears. Nothing will matter or work if we cannot—or will not—learn how to respectfully converse with one another, striving for understanding and mutuality.

We find in Paul's letter to the people in Ephesus a huge clue as to what we are meant to be about in the church:

> The gifts [Jesus] gave were that some would be apostles, some prophets, some evangelists, some pastors and teachers, to equip the saints for the work of ministry, for building up the body of Christ, until all of us come to the unity of the faith and of the knowledge of the Son of God, to maturity, to the measure of the full stature of Christ. We must no longer be children, tossed to and fro and blown about by every wind of doctrine, by people's trickery, by their craftiness in deceitful scheming. But speaking the truth in love, we must grow up in every way into him who is the head, into Christ, from whom the whole body, joined and knitted together by every ligament with which it is equipped, as each part is working properly, promotes the body's growth in building itself up in love.[25]

Our congregational leaders are there to equip us for the work of ministry, ministry that results in the building up of the congregation so that we *all* are unified in faith and in the knowledge of Jesus Christ, the Son of God. That unity then allows us to grow into the whole fullness of Christ. That fullness is also based on speaking the truth in love: the body of Christ, the congregation, grows and builds itself up in love . . . in respectful mutuality that can effect unity.

It takes work. It takes practice. Stop putting it off: begin today to prepare. As we acquire the skills we need to most effectively converse with folks—not merely talk about or speak to them—we will gain confidence and be able to defuse the ticking time bombs that threaten our survival. Transformation isn't possible without conversation. Holding environments are created in community, with others; nothing else is possible if we cannot converse with one another.

Notes

1. Starchaser, "Give a Man a Fish," Halfbakery, October 24, 1999, http://www.halfbakery.com/idea/Give_20A_20Man_20A_20Fish_2e_2e_2e#9680868 00.

2. Noah Weinberg, "48 Ways to Wisdom: Way 20, The Art Of Conversation," *Spirituality*, January 10, 2000, http://www.aish.com/spirituality/48ways/Way_20 _The_Art_of_Conversation.asp.

3. Loren Ekroth, "To Be, or Not," *Better Conversations*, e-mail newsletter, July 5, 2005, loren@conversation-matters.com.

4. Ibid.

5. Loren Ekroth, "The Fiction of Independent Conversation," *Better Conversations*, e-mail newsletter, July 5, 2005, loren@conversation-matters .com.

6. Ibid.

7. Leviticus 19:16.

8. Proverbs 16:28.

9. Dictionary.com.

10. Romans 1:30.

11. For examples, see 1 Timothy 3:11, 2 Timothy 3:3, and Titus 2:3.

12. Matthew 16:19.

13. Matthew 10:16b.

14. Ruth N. Koch and Kenneth C. Haugk, *Speaking the Truth in Love: How to Be an Assertive Christian* (St. Louis: Stephen Ministries, 1992), 7.

15. Ekroth, "The Fiction of Independent Conversation."

16. Mortimer J. Adler, "Some Rules For Good Conversation," Radical Academy, 1997, http://radicalacademy.com/adlerconversation.htm.

17. These statements and suggestions are slightly edited versions of those made by Mortimer Adler in "Some Rules for Good Conversation."

18. Adler, "Some Rules For Good Conversation."

19. Ekroth, "To Be, or Not."

20. Ekroth, "The Fiction of Independent Conversation."

21. You can go to http://www.conversationcafe.org to find a Conversation Café.

22. "Agreements and Process," Conversation Café, http://conversationcafe.org/Process%20and%20Agreements.htm, accessed August 14, 2008.

23. "Talk to Strangers?" Conversation Café, http://www.conversationcafe.org/Talk%20to%20Strangers.htm, accessed August 14, 2008.

24. 1 Corinthians 13:4–8a.

25. Ephesians 4:11–16.

10

At any moment, a twelve-step meeting of some sort or another is gathering in some part of the world. If you talk to someone working the steps, they will likely tell you that the first three steps are the foundation on which all the other steps, and recovery itself, build. Those first three steps are:

1. We admitted we were powerless . . . that our lives had become unmanageable.

2. We came to believe that a Power greater than ourselves could restore us to sanity.

3. We made a decision to turn our will and our lives over to the care of God *as we understood [God]*.[1]

More succinctly, some have condensed these three steps to: "I can't; God can; I think I'll let God." How I wish we in the church might learn and believe and trust in those three little—yet explosively powerful—statements.

I Can't

Congregational leadership in North America these days brings with it an incredibly heavy mantle. As we find ourselves in congregations that are facing decisions of life and death, we can easily shift into overachievement mode, doing everything of which we can possibly think to turn things around. We do not want the ship to go down on our watch, so we spend more time planning, more time cajoling, and more time attempting to produce (or even manipulate) results . . . often to no avail. Many of us find our reputations and our egos on the line. Pastors face a double-edged sword: sinking ships mean shrinking salaries (which few of us can afford) and we will do almost anything to avoid the uncomfortable position of having to justify our declining numbers to those to whom we are responsible . . . as though the numbers (up or down) are our sole responsibility.

In reality, "the numbers" are *not* our sole responsibility. One of the biggest mistakes churches make (and traps into which pastors allow themselves to fall) is hiring pastor-saviors. I have sat in several interviews where I have been asked questions like, "What programs (or ministries) have you developed that you'll bring here with you?" and "How will you help us grow?" As an interviewee, it is easy to see this as an open door to promote yourself and to make an impression that will help you last beyond your "competition." But questions of this nature are good indicators that the congregation is looking for a savior in a mortal body, a search that often later leads to great disappointment and belabored blame.

It is useful, and accurate, to state and reiterate that, while instrumental, pastors cannot solve a church's problems. Statistics show that attendance and membership numbers may surge in the first two to three years of a new pastorate; but those increases are not usually sustained, at least not because of the pastor. Actually, the numbers are merely a manifestation, a thermometer of sorts, of how well we are—or are not—traversing transformation's transitional journey, a journey that is meant to be shared by each participant in a congregation. But more than that, the journey does not belong to the congregation alone; it is, in fact, first and foremost God's.

A great many of us operate with an independent streak, as if we have all the answers and as if those answers rest solely on us. We have either lost, or never learned, the need to rely on God. Walk into most mainline church board meetings in the United States and you will find little difference between their agendas and those of most corporate board meetings, except, perhaps, for the requisite opening and closing parentheses of prayer. We use parliamentary procedures because, goodness forbid, we appear to be incapable of conducting the "business" of the church in a loving, respectful, Christ-like way. Indeed, holding a meeting in a room of the church seems to set off something in some of us that causes us to act less professional than we do when conducting our secular affairs.

I remember one such man at one of the churches I pastored. He was quite a successful businessman with a reputation for sound business practices. I know that he would never conduct his business affairs the way he conducted himself in the church's board meetings, where he was loud and obnoxious, and consistently wrested control of the meeting to keep things off-track (often leading to three- to five-hour board meetings). In fact, one of the early moves we made after my arrival was to reconfigure the meeting environment, invoking parliamentary procedure and asking people to come to a microphone to speak. In another setting, I have experienced members appealing to parliamentary procedure in an effort to move to a vote before hearing a word from the pastor. I wish I could say these were isolated events, but I continually get to see them repeated in church after church after church.

Many of our congregations set up our boardrooms in theater-style seating where we get to see our elected leaders' faces and the back of the head of the person sitting in front of us. The sheer size of the boards in many of our congregations prevent us from sitting in circles, knee-to-knee, so to speak, without space—physical, emotional, spiritual, and otherwise—between us. Our own reticence and need for space prevent such intimacy in congregations where this could be possible. But it is that kind of intimacy that allows us to move beyond "our" work and "our" ways of thinking to God's work and God's ways of thinking.

Few congregations know what it means to congregationally seek God and God's guidance, to "listen" for God's "voice" and proceed from that direction. Rather, we have been taught to jump onto the next program or idea or solution that sounds logical and good. In fact, many of you reading the first sentence of this paragraph may have no idea what it means; and others will find it to be absolutely ridiculous.

Several years ago, Dr. Charles M. Olsen introduced what has become known as worshipful work, an effort to ground the work of God in spirituality and worship.[2] Grounding God's work—the work of the church—in God demands that we seek God's guidance and grace, and it calls for a measure of reliance on God. Relying on God's guidance is not easy and basically depends on how well we are able to engage the process of tapping into God's Spirit; this process is called _discernment._

The Center for Transforming Religious Leadership defines discernment as "seeking the deepest yearnings of God's heart for us and for our communities. It is the gift of the Spirit. It must be noticed, accepted, treasured, and surrendered to if it is to be received. Communal discernment is an experience of group prayer and reflection on God's word."[3]

Discernment means setting aside our personal wants and wishes to allow for God's wants and wishes. It means assenting to the possibility that God wants a say in what we are doing. It means "letting go and letting God." And it starts with "We can't."

My husband is fond of the quote, "Pray like it all depends on God, work like it all depends on you."[4] The apostle James reminds us that faith and works go hand in hand: "faith by itself, if it is not accompanied by action, is dead."[5] Unfortunately, many of us on the transformational journey rely on our works more than on our faith. We somehow forget that we belong to God through Jesus Christ and that because of that relationship we are heirs to a great many promises. Many of us preach or hear this message most Sundays, but our congregations—maybe even we—are having a little trouble believing and living it.

Several years ago I divided a group of elders (the designated "spiritual leaders" of the church) into smaller groups of four and asked each group to share among themselves a joy and/or a challenge they had encountered in their experience as elders during the previous month. I told them that after they had finished sharing, I wanted them to stay in their small groups and pray for one another about those joys and challenges (and any other way the Holy Spirit might lead them to pray).

138

At the time, I was the youngest person in the room by ten years; some of those elders had been elders for nearly as long as I was old. That's probably why I was a little surprised by the nervous giggles at my request. I quickly summarized what I had just said and asked if there were any questions. "You want us to pray in our small groups?" one of the eldest elders asked. "Yes," I replied.

As I listened into their conversations around the room, I realized that nearly half the groups were unable to stay on topic. "Remember: share at least one joy and/or a challenge," I reminded them, "and then move into prayer."

Fifteen or twenty minutes into the exercise, several of the groups were moving into prayer. Three others were giggling and still way off topic. I suggested that the groups who had not yet started praying might want to start. Another elder asked, "You want us to pray, pastor?" "Yes," I answered (again). "You mean, you aren't going to pray?" "No," I tried to half-joke back, "y'all are."

I could tell his group was quite uncomfortable with the request and later learned that the elders there had never been asked or expected to do much more praying than at the communion table on Sunday morning, neither with each other nor with those for whom they were responsible.

As I recount that story, I once again find myself sad on several levels. I am sad because there are still elders in their sixties and seventies who have not been taught or expected to pray beyond rote prayers. I am sad because many of our pastors are unable to pray much more than someone else's "paragraph prayers" they've memorized or are reading out of a book. I am sad because we in the church have perpetuated the myth that our futures and the fate of our families, the church's future, and the fate of the world somehow depend on us as pastors (or on us as congregations) and that somehow *we* can make everything all right, even though we do not have the tools to rely on divine guidance. I am sad because we have not given people the tools or the resources to seek God with all their heart, soul, mind, and strength. And I am sad because we have failed to connect people with the God of hope and possibility.

We might wonder how many times those elders—perhaps we—have heard the words of Psalm 121 without claiming them as our own:

I lift up my eyes to the hills—from where will my help come? My help comes from the Lord, who made heaven and earth. He will not let your foot be moved; he who keeps you will not slumber. He who keeps Israel will neither slumber nor sleep. The Lord is your keeper; the Lord is your shade at your right hand. The sun shall not strike you by day, nor the moon by night. The Lord will keep you from all evil; he will keep your life. The Lord will keep your going out and your coming in from this time on and forevermore.

And how many times have you cried out the words from Psalm 40? Read them here and think of how helpful they may be for you or your congregation:

LORD, don't hold back your tender mercies from me. My only hope is in your unfailing love and faithfulness. For troubles surround me—too many to count! They pile up so high I can't see my way out. They are more numerous than the hairs on my head. I have lost all my courage. Please, LORD, rescue me! Come quickly, LORD, and help me.[6]

We hear the Older Testament stories like those of Joseph and Moses who are able to say, "I can't," one of the scariest but most freeing statements ever uttered. "I cannot interpret your dream," Joseph said to Pharaoh, "but God can.[7] God came to Moses and asked him to speak to yet another Pharaoh, now demanding the release of a nation of people: "I can't do it! I'm no orator. Why should Pharaoh listen to me?" Moses protests.[8] But we know now—as Moses soon discovered—that all things are possible with God.

We twenty-first-century Christians in the Western world find ourselves far removed from the stories and certainties of our faith. Not only are we disconnected from the faith stories of the Bible, we are disconnected from our own stories. Many of us have forgotten why in the first place we professed Jesus as our God and Saviour. Many more of us have never had to—or have never been taught to, or have never taken the time to—rely on the assurances that come with that profession. And so, now, as we find ourselves sinking into the miry depths of despair and desperation, we are hard pressed to call out to, let alone upon, God and our divine Saviour. In many respects, we have traded the truth of God for a lie, or for multiple mistruths, as we have relied on ourselves and forgotten that God's realm is not a matter of talk, but of "living by God's power."[9] We have forgotten that the ability to "do all things," comes only when Jesus Christ is strengthening us.[10]

GOD CAN

Beyond our inclination to be self-sufficient and successful, we tend to carry at least two misconceptions that get in the way of letting God be God and allowing God to do those things that only God can do. One of those misconceptions is that God can't; the other is that God won't.

Over the years culture and secular thinking have generally effaced God's abilities, even to the extent that professor of religion J. J. Altizer could popularly argue in the 1960s that "God has died in our cosmos, in our history, in our [existence]."[11] It is no secret that God is still doing great works—some would call them miracles—around the world but that we in the Western Hemisphere tend to rationalize them or dismiss them as preposterous stories or the delusions of people who are not as learned, refined, or "progressive" as ourselves.[12] A God who can create the heavens and the earth and change the patterns of nature and the course of history is beyond imagination. Week after week, thousands of people stand and profess the Apostles' Creed:

> I believe in God the Father Almighty,
>> maker of heaven and earth;
>
> And in Jesus Christ his only Son our Lord:
>> who was conceived by the Holy Spirit,
>>> born of the Virgin Mary,
>>> suffered under Pontius Pilate,
>>> was crucified, dead, and buried,
>>> he descended into hell;

the third day he rose from the dead;
he ascended into heaven,
    and sitteth at the right hand of God the Father Almighty;
from thence he shall come to judge the quick and the dead.

I believe in the Holy Spirit,
    the holy catholic church,
    the communion of saints,
    the forgiveness of sins,
    the resurrection of the body,
    and the life everlasting. Amen.[13]

But based on hundreds of conversations over the past twenty years, I have to wonder how many of us really believe what we profess. Often I hear more discussion about what we don't, or don't want to, believe. Some may think there is more to debate in those denominations and churches that are creedal or hold to articles of faith: the virginity of Jesus' mother, Mary; whether or not Jesus descended into hell and why; whether or not our bodies will be resurrected, and when; and if life really is eternal.

Yet even in my own Disciples denomination—wherein we claim to have "no creed but Christ" and most of our congregations exchange creeds such as the Apostles' or the Nicene for the simple statement "I believe that Jesus is the Son of the Living God and accept him as my Lord and Savior"—we can spend a lot of time arguing about what it means to believe and accept Jesus and about whether or not the world needs a Savior (or just some of us). It seems that when we do take time to think about what we believe, it's often easy to reduce God to what *we* think or perceive, removing our considerations beyond the realm of scripture and tradition. It's as though we've "progressed" into a higher way of thinking that negates centuries, and often sister churches' ways—of understanding. It's a short leap from what we think to what we perceive God can and cannot do.

Then there are those of us who truly believe that God won't, that for some reason God has rescinded God's promises to work all things "together for good for those who love God, who are called according to his purpose."[14] The author of the Newer Testament letter to the Hebrews reminds us that because

> [16]Human beings, of course, swear by someone greater than themselves, and an oath given as confirmation puts an end to all dispute. [17]In the same way, when God desired to show even more clearly to the heirs of the promise the unchangeable character of his purpose, he guaranteed it by an oath, [18]so that through two unchangeable things, in which it is impossible that God would prove false, we who have taken refuge might be strongly encouraged to seize the hope set before us. [19]We have this hope, a sure and steadfast anchor of the soul. . . [15]

Maybe we need to hear that promise in a new way. Try Eugene Peterson's translation:

> When God wanted to guarantee his promises, he gave his word, a rock-solid guarantee—God *can't* break his word. And because his word cannot change, the promise is likewise unchangeable.

> We who have run for our very lives to God have every reason to grab the promised hope with both hands and never let go. It's an unbreakable spiritual lifeline, reaching past all appearances right to the very presence of God.[16]

Can you hear those words: "a rock-solid guarantee . . . God *can't* break his word. . . . the promise is likewise unchangeable. . . . we have every reason to grab the promised hope with both hands and never let go. . ."?

I attended a board meeting one night as the board members were considering an incredible opportunity that would boost their ministry potential. On the downside, the opportunity would necessitate adding a staff person and an additional $50,000 to their budget. During a rather intense meeting, one of the board members sitting near me said, "It'll take a miracle to raise $50,000." I quietly replied, "God is still in the miracle business." The pastor had made sure they spent extended and concentrated time that evening praying for discernment and for their needs, fears, and frustrations as board members and representatives of the congregation. Some thought that was a waste of time.

Four weeks later, the congregation had accounted for $47,000 of the needed $50,000! The pastor kept that fact in front of the leadership and the congregation for some time as a reminder that God is, indeed, still answering prayers. Yet not more than four months later, the same board member again observed in a meeting that the kind of opportunities they were considering that evening could only be accomplished via a miracle. The pastor reminded him that they had been miracle benefactors not even six months earlier; but, while the board member acknowledged that as a fact, he told the pastor with all sincerity that miracles are rare and the church would not be seeing any more of them.

Hmmmmm. . . . Is it that God won't, or that we won't get out of God's way?

I THINK I'LL LET GOD

If we are faithful with a little, God will give us more. And when we are faithful with the more, God trusts us with even more than that. It is a fact. It has happened for centuries, and it is happening in churches around the world today. But the converse of that is true as well: if we are not faithful with whatever we have, we cannot expect God to give us more.

Yet faithfulness is not one of our buzzwords in the church. We go to worship on Sundays (or some other time), but what we hear and profess often has little bearing on how we live our lives once we leave the building. We pull out of the church parking lot and drive like banshees to the restaurant down the road so we can get seated before the folks from the other churches get there . . . and then we snip at our servers and notoriously undertip. One of the most embarrassing moments in my life was standing with a clergy colleague who made sure everyone in earshot knew she was a minister as she argued maliciously with an airline representative after our flight had been delayed because of weather. We argue with one another. We rip our pastors and each other as though we were shredding paper. We ignore, justify, or otherwise refuse to wrestle with the parts of the Bible that make us uncomfortable. And we do not love the Lord our God with all our hearts, souls, minds, or strength. Don't believe it? The evidence is all around us.

Far too commonly in larger towns and cities we can find ads selling church buildings. In some of those cases, the congregation has outgrown the building. In other cases, such as in this ad from *The Source* (the newspaper of the Church Council of Greater Seattle), the building has outgrown the congregation:

QUEEN ANNE CHURCH FOR SALE

Dramatic church building in a prime Queen Anne location available for sale for the first time since its construction in 1926. This property recently appraised for over $3,000,000 but is being offered at $2,300,000.[17]

I cannot help but draw a parallel between that ad and an account recorded in the Older Testament's 2 Kings. In 2 Kings 16 we read about Ahaz, the king of Judah, who reigned 735–715 BCE. We are told that King Ahaz "did not do what was right in the sight of the LORD his God, as his ancestor David had done, but he "walked in the ways of the kings of Israel."[18] Like his counterparts in Israel, Ahaz adopted many of the practices and religious notions of the nations around him. Indeed, on a trip to Damascus to meet with the king of Assyria, King Ahaz spotted the ornate Damascus altar on which the Damascenes had made pagan sacrifices. He sent a sketch of the altar to his priest Uriah and asked Uriah to build one just like it.

When King Ahaz got back home, his new altar was sitting prominently in front of God's temple, shadowing the bronze altar that generations earlier King Solomon had built and dedicated to God. To make matters worse, Ahaz moved God's altar from its specifically positioned place and directed Uziah to begin using the new pagan altar for all God's offerings while Ahaz would use God's bronze altar for the pagan practice of inquiry.[19] As if this wasn't bad enough, King Ahaz then began to pillage and dismantle the parts of God's sanctuary that were offensive to the king of Assyria.

For just a moment, let's hold this in contrast with 2 Kings 17, where we are told that Judah's counterpart, the Israelites, lost their land, their treasures, their freedom, their inheritance, all that they held dear because they repeatedly "sinned against the Lord their God" (verse 7). Like Judah, they did not love God with the whole of their beings. They did not take to heart the commandments God had given. They did not impress those commandments on their children. They did not talk about God or God's will and ways when sitting at home, when walking along the road, when lying down, and when getting up.[20] They disrespected God's sanctuary. And they lost *everything*.

Although King Ahaz's desecration of the temple and disregard for God's commands were tantamount to the sins of the Israelites, God spared Ahaz and Judah (at least for the time being). Their reprieve, however, came only because Ahaz's son, Hezekiah, was a person after God's own heart, who

> held fast to the LORD; he did not depart from following him but kept the commandments that the Lord commanded Moses. The Lord was with him; wherever he went, he prospered. He rebelled against the king of Assyria and would not serve him.[21]

Hezekiah was faithful with the little he inherited and turned it into a lot.

Today, many of us find ourselves dismantling and selling off parts—if not the whole—of our, God's, sanctuaries. We sell our communion sets and the extra dishes and chairs for a trifle to make ends meet because we perceive we will never have enough people to use them again. Empty churches that once hosted revivals with still acclaimed speakers are fodder for rodents and insects. Could it be that somewhere in our histories we were not faithful with the little, or the more, that we had been given? Is it possible that we could meet our ends if we could figure out how to mean what we say and say what we mean and do what we hear on Sundays and beyond? Might we, like Judah, get to relish a reprieve if we could find ways to surrender ourselves and give over to God the whole of our very beings? Perhaps if we might reprioritize our lives—become like Hezekiah, a person after God's own heart—not only would our lives be dramatically different, but so might the lives of our churches. Yet many, perhaps most, of us separate our personal lives from the life of the churches we attend.

Few of us know what the Ten Commandments are, let alone know where to find them; and we don't understand that to be a problem. The same holds true for the two Great Commandments and the Great Commission, the latter of which we tend to forsake because the "e-word," evangelism, tends to challenge our reticence to talk about God and is often a symptom of our not conversing with God. Though we are watching a rise in interest in spirituality, many of us are spending a lot of time reading and talking about it rather than conversing with the Spirit and listening for God's "voice," let alone following God's direction.

The signs of congregational decline and disaster are all around. Our financial reserves are eroding. We find ourselves selling our land, our buildings, our treasures. Our choices are compromising our freedom of choice about whom we can hire and retain. We are having to choose between building maintenance, programming, missions, and denominational support. We are hosting more funerals than baptisms. Our congregations are at serious risk of folding, if not soon then in the next ten to twenty years. Forget about thriving; many of us are barely surviving. And quite basically, the prevention of death rests in whether or not we as individuals and congregations can let God be God.

REMEMBER WHO YOU ARE AND WHOSE YOU ARE

Like it or not, we are merely mortal; and mortality is a limiting factor. We are literally driving ourselves insane and making ourselves physically sick trying to be everything to everybody. I love when friends remind me that I need a Savior, not to be one.

In many respects, our ability to defuse our congregational time bombs rests in truthfulness and trust. Can we be truthful with ourselves . . . and with those with whom we are journeying? Are we able to admit that we don't have all the answers? Can we become open to the freedom that comes when we stop working as though everything depends on us? And how ready are we—are you—to really *trust* God anyhow? Truthfulness is the foundation of trust. We are not able to trust, or even contemplate trust, until we can get truthful with ourselves and admit that we cannot transform our congregations, unless we can assent to the fact that there is One who can . . . and that One is God. Then we have to figure out together how to let God be God: in our lives and in the life of our churches.

Figuring that out, how to let God be God, is grounded in remembering who we are and whose we are; and that remembering is relative to our staying actively engaged with the One who has sought us and bought us. How do we do that? By finding ways to move—perhaps ourselves, perhaps our churches—past the rote and parenthetical prayers (you know, those short little prayers at the opening and closing of meetings and worship services). Prayer in whatever form works best for you allows us to move into places where we can hear God *and* be open to expectantly anticipate and experience God's almighty presence, Jesus' unparalleled power, and the Holy Spirit's miraculous movement. For some of us, that comes in silence. For others of us, that comes from walking a labyrinth or manipulating prayer beads. Yet others of us have to sing or dance. The ways to encounter God, Jesus, and the Holy Spirit are as diverse as we are. Once in their presence, though, we begin to find those ways to allow God to be God in our lives and in the lives of our churches.

But first, we may need to do a little soul searching and come back to acknowledging and wrestling with what it means that God is God and Jesus Christ is Sovereign in our lives:

> So acknowledge today and take to heart that the LORD is God in heaven above and on the earth beneath; there is no other. Keep his statutes and his commandments, which I am commanding you today for your own well-being and that of your descendants after you, so that you may long remain in the land that the LORD your God is giving you for all time.[22]

Discovering and recovering who we are on the inside, who we are in Jesus Christ, depends on our ability to avail ourselves of prayer, learning, and discerning how we "hear" from God. When we discover, develop, and strengthen who we are in the One whose we are, we will find ourselves grounded in the areas that are necessary to hold all the environments necessary to survive the transformational journey. And we will find our lives, the lives of our congregations, and the lives of those with whom we journey transforming and transformational.

It is as short and as simple as this. The secret to transformation is not about finances, administration, and program. It is first and foremost about God and our relationship with God. We know that God can do all things and we have been taught that we, too, can do all things through Christ who strengthens us.[23] We may not have majored in bomb disposal, disarmament, or detonation but we can rest assured that if we will seek God with all our heart, soul, mind, and strength, God will guide and provide for whatever task God sets in front of us . . . even defusing the bombs in our congregations. Indeed, the future of our congregations, of the church, depends on it.

Notes

1. Alcoholics Anonymous, "The Twelve Steps Of Alcoholics Anonymous," http://www.aa.org/en_information_aa.cfm?PageID=17&SubPage=68.

2. Worshipful-Work: Center for Transforming Religious Leadership, "The Basics," http://www.worshipful-work.org/about_us.html.

3. Worshipful-Work: Center for Transforming Religious Leadership, "Home Page," http://www.worshipful-work.org.

4. This is a popular version of the quote attributed to Francis Cardinal Spellman (1889–1967): "Pray as if everything depended upon God and work as if everything depended upon man." The Quotations Page, "Quotation Details: Quotation #2816," http://www.quotationspage.com/quote/2816.html.

5. James 2:17, NIV.

6. Psalm 40:11–13, The Holy Bible New Living Translation (NLT) (Carol Stream, IL: Tyndale House Publishers, 1996).

7. Genesis 41:15–16.

8. Exodus 6:30, NLT.

9. 1 Corinthians 4:20, NLT and NIV.

10. Philippians 4:13, The Holy Bible New King James Version (NKJV) (Nashville: Thomas Nelson, 1982).

11 Patrick Gray, "Religion: 'God Is Dead' Controversy," *The New Georgia Encyclopedia*, April 1, 2003, http://www.georgiaencyclopedia.org/nge/Article.jsp?path=/Religion/HistoricalEventsMovements&id=h-861.

12. For a fascinating discussion on the phenomenal movement of God in the world today, see C. Peter Wagner's *Acts of the Holy Spirit: A Modern Commentary on the Book of Acts* (Ventura, CA: Regal Books, 2000).

13. "The Apostles' Creed," traditional version, *The United Methodist Hymnal* (Nashville: United Methodist Publishing House, 1989), 881.

14. Romans 8:28, NKJV.

15. Hebrews 6:16–19a.

16. Hebrews 6:17–19a, Eugene Peterson, *The Message: the Bible in Contemporary Language* (Colorado Springs: NavPress, 2002).

17. Church Council of Greater Seattle, *The Source*, no. 287 (September 2005), 8.

18. 2 Kings 16:2–3.

19. 2 Kings 16:15.

20. See Deuteronomy 6:4–9.

21. 2 Kings 18:6–7.

22. Deuteronomy 4:39–40.

23. See Philippians 4:13.

AFTERWORD

They say the end is in the beginning and, according to Dan Wilson, who penned the 1998 song *Closing Time*, "every new beginning comes from some other beginning's end." So here we find ourselves at a beginning. If you take nothing else away from this book, please take these final four observations.

First, whether we choose to be or not, we are on a transformational journey. Life is not static; it is one of continual transformation, so whether we are talking about human life or the life of a congregation, we are always in a state of transformation. Staying in the present is never an option; if we try to stay in the present, we will sooner or later find ourselves in the past. We can choose to ignore, fight, or make the most of the journey. I have found the journeying to be most fulfilling.

Second, you are not alone if you find yourself in a declining or struggling congregation, and you can find strength in journeying with others who are struggling too. But know that commiseration can be contagious and survival depends not on concentrating on the "good ol' days" or the way things "aren't"; survival demands action. There is also an emerging trend for pastors and congregations of struggling congregations to "try to figure it out" together, and I keep hearing more about "peer coaching" models. Too often, these are more like the blind leading the blind. There are trained consultants who can help; do not ignore them or think you cannot afford them. And do not let your denomination off the hook, either. As denominational staff positions come open, fill with them people who have formal training and experience in transformation (also known as revitalization, renewal, and transition). If you are fortunate enough to be on a search committee, ask questions about what the candidates have learned from their own experiences and what kind of "plan" they have to encourage and support transformation on a congregation-by-congregation basis. Don't delude yourself into thinking that someone with little or no experience or formal training has the necessary experience. Ask about candidates' experiences in a variety of settings (most of our judicatories comprise churches of all shapes and sizes in all kinds of settings . . . one size or program will not fit all!). How have they mentored pastors and congregational leaders to be what God is calling them to be? Ask them about their faith journey and listen for the ways they rely on God. What kind of prayer and spiritual disciplines do they use? How do they take care of themselves?

And when you find that special someone who is striving to love God with the whole of his or her very being (I say striving because I am not sure that that kind of love is completely possible on the human side of eternity) and has the experience needed for such a task as this, be sure to afford that person time for retreat and renewal in addition to four weeks of vacation and time for continuing education . . . and hold him or her accountable for taking it. Accept no excuses: spiritual leadership and God's work are painstakingly arduous and require long hours with people, in study, but most importantly with God.

Third, engage congregational transformation carefully. Please be careful about jumping on one bandwagon or another. Some will advise, "Just do something," but please, please, please do not do anything either too quickly or too slowly. As our financial and human resources decrease, congregational enthusiasm and energy erode as well. These are not easily renewable resources and are running low in many of our congregations. Be careful.

Fourth and foremost, if you want to survive the transformational journey, do not engage it without first having in place holding environments for change, those relationships and resources that allow us to face the changes and challenges transformation brings without succumbing to the despairing depths that come when we are in survival mode. This book has discussed the ten basic holding environments that can make the difference between successfully walking the transformational journey and congregational death.

These holding environments are essential tools for defusing our congregational time bombs; and they emerge when Christians and congregations practice the "Four Greats." The safety, strength, health, vitality, and vibrancy of our congregations rest in these basic Four Greats; it doesn't matter whether your congregation hosts six, sixty, six hundred, or six thousand people for worship on a weekly basis. Regardless of size or age, every congregation has at least a few time bombs ticking away. Our ability to defuse our time bombs and survive accidental bomb blasts rests in our ability to shift our foci from inward to outward as we practice the Greats, accepting Jesus' Great Invitation to follow him and then honestly and with integrity living into both of the Great Commandments: (a) to love God first and foremost with the whole of our being and (b) to focus our love, God's love, on others. Of course, we cannot forget the Great Commission and its directive to "go out."

Explicitly, each of the preceding chapters correlates to the Great Commandments and Great Commission and specifies the various essential holding environments, as shown in Table 1, on page 154.

I have chosen to end the chapters with the first part of the Great Commandment, believing that true transformation is not possible unless it is grounded in, and guided by, God. Indeed, although I understand Great Commandment "B" and the Great Commission to be equal in importance to Great Commandment "A," I am reticent to say they are inherently possible unless we love God with the whole of our very beings; genuinely loving our neighbors and going out to baptize and disciple others are nearly impossible, at least for the long haul, without loving God to the best of our abilities.

I long for the day when churches as a whole are able to move past their fears and anxieties to become places of welcome, acceptance, and respect. I long for the evenings when our boards and committees will

Table 1

CHAPTER	HOLDING ENVIRONMENT	"GREAT" CORRELATION
10	Remember who you are and whose you are	Great Commandment A
9	Practice the fine art of conversation	Great Commandment B
8	Be a hospital for sinners, not a hotel for saints	Great Commandment B
7	Play together to stay together	Great Commandment B
6	Stay on course	Great Commission
5	Keep cool, calm, and collected	Great Commission
4	Put the right people in the right places	Great Commission
3	Find the right fits	Great Commission
2	Take what you need	Great Commission
1	Face your money fears	Great Commission

spend more time rejoicing, thinking expectantly, and anticipatorily planning for the future than we currently do on financial woes, program approvals and disapprovals, and matters associated with poor conflict management. I look forward to the time when we will consistently celebrate consensus rather than having to remember the ins and outs of Roberts Rules and how to count votes and quorums. Conversations about what we can do to attract whom are so much more life-giving than when we talk about who will like or dislike what. Consciously surrendering our control to God and waiting to speak when we have clarity about what

God is trying to do with and through us is much more respectful and honoring than when we allow the anxieties of one or a few to guide and control our meetings.

Becoming grounded in our love for God and others and getting a better understanding of what it means to love ourselves will allow us to defuse the time bombs that threaten our transformational journeys. And once they are out of the way, we will be able to get real about how to we are going to effectively go out, baptize, teach, and make disciples.

The more holding environments we have in place, the smoother our transitional journeys will be. Start small, but start at the beginning. Take seriously the warnings from Psalm 127:1—"Unless the LORD builds the house, those who build it labor in vain. Unless the LORD guards the city, the guard keeps watch in vain."

But know that unless your congregation is also one made up of people who love one another and help people to love themselves, your transformational efforts will be debilitating, if not deadly.

In my position as a judicatory minister, I am often called to consult with congregations who are in the last throes of death, often because of one too many bomb blasts. I find myself saying increasingly often, "Please call me before you don't know how to pay your pastor's salary or next month's mortgage. Please call me before you don't know how you're going to fill your quota for elders or deacons. Please call me so we can move beyond surviving to thriving. Please call me so you can stop wandering around in the desert in survival mode and become more effective at helping folks find God's realm."

I make some churches mad. They'd rather not hear that at their current rate of spending (already streamlined with a less-than-part-time pastor) they will run completely out of money in five, four, even three years. None of us wants to hear that what we're doing may not be "effective," and even I find it painful to be critiqued.

Recently I have begun to use a chart that helps people look at where they are on a continuum of effectiveness or transformation (see Table 2, page 156). Museum churches, those that are grounded in the past and are consumed by the throes of survival, are doing next to nothing that is significantly transforming themselves or their neighbors. Maintenance

Table 2. A Continuum of Congregational Effectiveness and Transformation[31]

1 → MUSEUM	2 → MAINTENANCE	3 → MOVING	4 → MOMENTUM	5 MISSIONING
Tried & True (but often Tired)	**Transitioned** (often think "we've arrived")	**Transient** (exploring different programs and ministries)	**Transitional** (moving from exploring to clarity about what to do)	**Transforming** (having influence congregationally on the community/world)
With few exceptions, worship with only one or two generations present	Stable or declining	Often "growing"	Size doesn't matter	Can be larger OR small
Survival is a key	Survival is still pressing	Plans are made with a future orientation	The move from good to great is on	Strive for greatness and excellence
Keepers of what is and what was; the past is prominent	The past is prominent but the "now" is also important	Living in the present with a sense of future possibilities (the future isn't scary!)	Future oriented, with sensitivity to the present	Future and outward focus with a sensitivity to those within and without the church's doors … and those to come
Mission = ministry	Don't think in terms of mission and vision; status quo is important, usually for the sake of what is and with little about what could be	An awareness that mission is to be claimed and vision articulated	The church's mission and vision are articulated	Mission and vision guide decisions about ministry development
Mission, if any, generally exists as financial giving, often to local or "pet" projects and sometimes to the denomination	May be a little more involved in mission than a museum church, but giving (rather than "going out") to outside causes is most common	Ministries and mission are generally good and solid, but there is an awareness that they can be better	Ministries and mission are developed in light of mission and vision; signature ministry (or ministries) is/are being developed	One of the church's ministries/missions is serving as a model and teaching congregation for other pastors and churches
Faithful to those who are present	The satisfaction of individuals in the congregation is key	Increasing awareness of the needs and satisfaction of individuals outside the congregation	Momentum comes from asking and discerning what God wants the congregation to be and to do	Consistently and continuously engage ministry reflection and evaluation and, when necessary, redirection

churches are in much the same boat, although they are likely engaging ministries that may be making an impression on those who come weekly, but likely not on those who live in the community. Moving churches are (becoming) aware that God has a purpose for them. Momentum churches are motivated and beginning to live into intentional planning that is strategically grounded in what God is calling them to be and do. Missioning churches, then, are those that continually plan, evaluate, re-develop ministries and redirect resources as necessary, and intentionally live as God is calling them to be and do. I once heard the Rev. Rick Frost say, "A truly great church is one that is living out the Great Commandments and Great Commission."[1] Indeed, a truly great church is one that provides environments where God can be experienced and explored in ways that allow personal transformations to occur and allow we who are being transformed to be equipped, empowered, and encouraged to engage in nothing less than God's work of transforming others, our communities, and the world.

Think about your congregation for a moment. Whose life has been transformed, truly changed, because of your congregation? What is his or her name? How did his or her life change? How does his or her life continue to transform? What about others?

Often when we talk about transformation, we talk about it in terms of becoming "transformed." It's time we move past the notion that we will ever be "transformed." Rather, we owe it to our churches and to God's realm to become transformational places. Though that may sound like a matter of semantics, the focus on congregations "needing to be transformed" exacerbates one of our historic problems as congregations: an inward focus. To say, however, that congregations need to be, or become, places of transformation puts the focus back where it belongs: beyond "us." It posits that congregations are meant to be places that transform lives: within and outside our doors . . . that we're meant to be those hospitals for sinners rather than hotels that are harboring saints.

The transition to being transformational is one of the toughest commitments you will ever make and it *is* fraught with time bombs. But the reality is, whether or not you engage the transformational journey, you already have some bombs in place (you may just not hear them ticking yet).

Know, though, that you can survive the journey. You will, however, have to be grounded, committed, intentional, and strategic about it.

Perhaps you have resonated with *Top 10 Ways to Defuse Your Congregational Time Bomb.* Perhaps I have made you angry. At the very least I hope I have given you some ways to help you move beyond living in survival mode to a place where you can see options and know you have choices.

Indeed, that is my prayer:

May you hear the Spirit's encouragement.

May you feel the tangible touch of Jesus.

May you experience God's love and power in such ways that you will be not merely enlightened but empowered and equipped to forge ahead, out of the wildernesses.

May you truly thrive in your life and ministry and find joy . . . whether that be again or for the first time.

May you find others with whom to journey: friends and companions with whom to converse, laugh, play, and pray . . . friends who will shield you from the blasts, bandage your wounds, and allow you to console, counsel, and care for them.

May you find health and life and live in such a way that others will be inspired and motivated to journey with you into God's realm.

And may together we delight in God's will and ways and love always in all ways.

Amen.

Notes

1. Rev. Rick Frost, recently retired as senior minister of Broadway Christian Church (Disciples of Christ) in Columbia, Missouri.

2. © J. Kristina Tenny-Brittian, 2007.

Additional Leadership Resources from The Pilgrim Press

Order today and receive 20 percent off retail price!

I Refuse to Lead a Dying Church!

Paul Nixon

Addresses key choices leadership in mainline churches must make in order for their churches to survive.

ISBN 978-0-8298-1759-1 / Paper / 128 pages / $17

Feed the Fire!

Avoiding Clergy Burnout

Bruce G. Epperly and Katherine Gould Epperly

Clergy physical, professional, and vocational health and well-being.

ISBN 978-0-8298-1795-9 / Paper / 176 pages / $22

Leadership for Vital Congregations

Congregational Vitality

Anthony B. Robinson

This book, the first in a new series of resources to guide clergy and lay leaders in creating vital congregations, focuses on leadership styles, approaches, and strategies.

ISBN 978-0-8298-1712-6 / Paper / 128 /pages / $12

Becoming a Pastor

Forming Self and Soul for Ministry

Jaco J. Hamman

Explores and defines the complicated work involved in actually becoming a pastor.

ISBN 978-0-8298-1749-2 / Paper / 192 pages / $22

FUNERALS WITH TODAY'S FAMILIES IN MIND
A Handbook for Pastors

Doreen M. McFarlane

Help for pastors facing the wide variety of complex family issues involved with today's funerals and memorial services.

ISBN 978-0-8298-1786-7 / Paper / 144 pages / $18

WEDDINGS WITH TODAY'S FAMILIES IN MIND
A Handbook for Pastors

Doreen M. McFarlane

A handbook for clergy on how to organize and perform traditional as well as nontraditional wedding ceremonies.

ISBN 978-0-8298-1737-9 / Paper / 128 pages / $18

HOW TO GET ALONG WITH YOUR CHURCH
Creating Cultural Capital for Doing Ministry

George B. Thompson Jr.

Ways in which pastors can invest themselves deeply into how their church does its work and ministries.

ISBN 0-8298-1437-X / Paper / 176 pages / $18

SOLOMON'S SUCCESS
Four Essential Keys to Leadership

Kenneth L. Samuel

Shares Solomon's four keys of leadership found in 1 Kings: wisdom, work, worship, and witness.

ISBN 978-0-8298-1572-6 / Paper / 112 pages / $15

ALLIGATORS IN THE SWAMP
Power, Ministry, and Leadership

George B. Thompson Jr., editor

Foreword by Andrew Young

Explores the issue of power and how it challenges ministry.

ISBN 0-8298-1671-2 / Paper / 208 pages / $21

CAN THIS CHURCH LIVE?
A Congregation, Its Neighborhood, and Social Transformation

Donald H. Matthews

The story of a church that struggled to survive within a changing community.

ISBN 0-8298-1648-8 / Paper / 112 pages / $14

HOPE IN CONFLICT
Discovering Wisdom in Congregational Turmoil

David R. Sawyer

Valuable church leadership tool that helps leaders identify and lead with hope in conflict.

ISBN 0-8298-1758-4 / Paper / 176 pages / $20

WHEN STEEPLES CRY
Leading Congregations through Loss and Change

Jaco J. Hamman

Proper mourning of loss and change in churches is a vital and life-giving aspect of healthy church leadership.

ISBN 0-8298-1694-1 / Paper / 192 pages / $21

To order these or any other books from The Pilgrim Press, call or write to:

THE PILGRIM PRESS
700 PROSPECT AVENUE
CLEVELAND, OH 44115-1100

Phone orders: 800.537.3394 (M–F, 8:30 AM – 4:30 PM ET)
Fax orders: 216.736.2206

Or order from our web site at www.thepilgrimpress.com

Please include shipping charges of $6 for the first book and $1 for each additional book.

When ordering by phone please use Promotion Code B101.

Prices subject to change without notice.